PRAISE FOR *CONNECTING WITH SUCCESS*

"*Connecting with Success* is as comprehensive as it is insightful. As a complete guide to menteeing, it covers every aspect of discovering and harnessing wisdom from another. From planning a strategy to becoming a mentor yourself, the book offers a cornucopia of valuable tips and techniques, as well as compelling processes and practices."

From the Foreword by Chip R. Bell, author of *Managers as Mentors*

"Kathleen Barton takes the mystery out of mentoring and networking. The practical steps and advice provided in this book are practiced by many professionals at PricewaterhouseCoopers. They can help you, too!"

Ann Rhoads, Partner, PricewaterhouseCoopers

"If you don't have a mentor and haven't a clue as to how to widen your network, let Kathleen Barton be your guide. Her book contains great wisdom and a plethora of how-to ideas. All are critical to career planning."

Beverly Kaye, author of *Up Is Not the Only Way*
and *Love 'Em or Lose 'Em*

"Kathleen Barton knows modern mentoring! She's done an excellent job of revealing proven strategies for landing the mentors and network contacts you need. You'll especially like and learn from the dozens of case studies and exercises she provides."

Linda Phillips-Jones, Ph.D., author of *The New Mentors and Proteges*

"Continuous development is a key to success in today's organizations. The examples, tools, and techniques in this book will enable you to enhance your career by building your own mentoring network."

Jim Robinson, coauthor of *Performance Consulting*

CONNECTING WITH SUCCESS

CONNECTING WITH SUCCESS

HOW TO BUILD A MENTORING NETWORK TO FAST-FORWARD YOUR CAREER

KATHLEEN BARTON

Davies-Black Publishing
Palo Alto, California

Published by Davies-Black Publishing, an imprint of Consulting Psychologists Press, Inc., 3803 East Bayshore Road, Palo Alto, CA 94303.

Special discounts on bulk quantities of Davies-Black books are avaiable to corporations, professional associatins, and other organizations. For details, contact the Director of Book Sales at Davies-Black Publishing, an imprint of Consulting Psychologists Press, Inc., 3803 East Bayshore Road, Palo Alto, CA 94303; 650-691-9123; fax 650-623-9271.

Visit the Davies-Black Publishing web site at www.daviesblack.com.

05 04 03 02 01 10 9 8 7 6 5 4 3 2 1
Printed in the United States of America

Library of Congress Cataloging-in-Publication Data
Barton, Kathleen
Connecting with success : how to build a mentoring network to fast-forward your career/ Kathleen Barton.—1st ed.
p. cm.
Includes bibliographical references and index.
ISBN 0-89106-162-2 (pbk.)
1. Mentoring in business. 2. Mentoring. 3. Business networks. 4. Career development. 5. Vocational guidance I. Title.

HF5385 .B37 2001
650.14—dc21

2001042366

FIRST EDITION
First printing 2001

CONTENTS

FOREWORD

When I was a young boy I used to go fishing with my granddaddy. It was the old-fashioned approach to fishing, complete with rowboat, cane poles, and large, slimy earthworms we coaxed from a swampy area near the fishpond. A man of few words, Granddaddy took his fishing very seriously.

"How come you catch so many more fish than I do?" I asked him one sunny day as he and I were trying to catch "a mess" as we called the sufficient quantity for supper.

"Son," he said rather sternly, without looking up, "You're not holding your mouth right!" Now for a six-year old, his glib response was a prelude to lots of facial contortions. But my catches never seemed to increase.

"Keep after him to teach you what he knows about fishing," advised my mother. I had just complained to her of my unsuccessful efforts to catch more fish even with my mouth held just right. I courageously asked a lot more questions of him, usually before we got into the boat, not after he got that fixed stare at the cork. The outcome was a mentee's bounty. His gruff "mouth-holding" advice turned out to really be code for an array of fishing know-how . . . like sitting still, being quiet, waiting until the cork had submerged, and setting the hook properly. After that, I vowed to be an unrelenting mentee.

Connecting with Success is about how to be an unrelenting mentee. It goes to the heart of what it means to be a successful learner in today's time's-up, learn-on-the-run world. As humans, we are genetically wired to grow. Research has shown that humans possess a kind of a "wisdom gene." Humans' growth-enhancing curiosity enabled them to successfully adapt en route to being the homo sapiens (wise ones) of the animal kingdom. That "wisdom gene" adaptation trait is a necessity in today's business world—perhaps more crucial even than transforming a bone into a tool was in prehistoric times.

Yet learning for success today is far more complex than the instinct-based learning of yesteryear. Today, what we know and can do becomes obsolete almost overnight. Former Royal Dutch Shell strategic planning guru Arie De Gies once wrote, "Your ability to learn faster than your competition is your only sustainable competitive advantage." While he was talking about companies, the message is just as relevant for individuals.

Today, confidence is as crucial to success as competence. Grace under pressure is lauded as an asset worthy of affirmation in most change-frenzied organizations. "In times of massive change," wrote philosopher Eric Hoffer, "it is the learner who will inherit the earth while the learned stay foolishly tied to a world that no longer exists." Learners see change as something to be confidently embraced, not timidly resisted. *Connecting with Success* is a prescription for confidence, what author Kathleen Barton labels "career self-reliance."

Today, access to mentors and learning opportunities is far more challenging. Mentees must cope with mergers, reorganizations, and downsizing almost weekly, changing mentors as well as remote sites and strange work times almost daily challenging mentor availability. It means that being unrelenting as a mentee must be combined with being clever. It suggests that networking skills are as vital as listening skills. And that is where this book becomes a powerful resource.

Success today requires a whole-brain approach. Analytical prowess must be balanced with relationship proficiency. The successful employee must possess emotional intelligence as well as logical acumen. To contribute to this pursuit of balance, *Connecting with Success* combines concrete checklists and how-to's with heartwarming stories of successful (and unsuccessful) mentoring relationships. The blend yields a path toward competence and confidence—in a word, success.

According to Homer's *The Odyssey,* when Odysseus left the Greek province he ruled to fight the Trojan War, he worried about who would be responsible for the tutelage of his only son (and heir). Telemachus was only twelve at the time and fast approaching adolescence. Odysseus selected an old family friend named Mentor to be Telemachus's teacher. Mentor was described as wise and sensitive. His name has been used ever since to refer to one charged with helping another learn.

As a mentor's mentor, Kathleen Barton brings wisdom (as one experienced with being both a mentor and a mentee) that enables her to "think" in mentoring. She also writes with a sensitive pen that yields a book that is pragmatic and compassionate, relevant and supportive. Mentors are strongly advised to review this book. It can help them "get in the mind of the mentee" in order to forge a partnership for learning.

This book is as comprehensive as it is insightful. As a complete guide to menteeing, it covers every aspect of discovering and harnessing wisdom from another. From planning a strategy to becoming a mentor yourself, the book offers a cornucopia of valuable tips and techniques, as well as compelling processes and practices. If there had been a six-year-old's version of this book in the early fifties, I might have caught a lot more fish with a lot less anxiety!

Chip R. Bell,
Author of *Managers as Mentors*

INTRODUCTION

What do the folllowing scenarios have in common?

COLETTE ADAMS

Engineer Colette Adams aspired to become an engineering manager, and she found a manager who was willing to serve as her mentor. He confirmed that she had what it takes to be a manager, and his opinion gave her confidence. Colette's mentor also helped her with her interviewing skills, and he put her in touch with other people who could help her. Nine months after initiating this mentoring relationship, Colette was promoted to manager. ■

As a customer service representative, Pete Sanchez listened to customers' complaints all day long. Feeling that the pay was not worth what he had to put up with, he started networking to find a new job. A family friend, Al, who was a manager at a

Fortune 100 electronics firm, told Pete about a telemarketing start-up operation in the company. Al thought that Pete, with his business degree and customer service experience, would be a good fit. He put Pete in touch with the hiring manager, and Pete landed the job. ▮

These two anecdotes have a common theme: They both involve people helping people and going out of their way to help others reach important goals. This kind of help can take the form of a long-term mentoring partnership or a one-time interaction. Whether you find a long- or short-term mentor or a one-time networking contact, mentors and networks serve the same purpose: helping you get ahead in your career.

You can gain knowledge and skills from a mentor and learn more quickly than you might on your own. Because mentors have been there, you can learn from their successes as well as from their mistakes. If you're new to an organization, a seasoned manager can help you understand the organization's culture and politics. He or she can help you learn how to get things done in the organizational system. A mentor provides advice, guidance, and support. Think of it as having your own personal coach. Your mentor is someone you can use to test your ideas, someone who can give you honest, constructive feedback. Ultimately, your mentor can help you achieve your career goals.

Networking gives you access to valuable knowledge and allows you to learn from others. When you have a good network, you know who can help you do what. You know where to go for the crucial information you need in order to do your job more quickly. Networking is especially important to salespeople and entrepreneurs: effective networking can bring potential clients and increase sales. Networking is effective because people prefer doing business with people they know.

Everyone, at every stage of a career, needs mentors and networks, and today mentors and networks are even more important than they were yesterday. For example, corporations are changing fast. Employees used to be able to rely on their companies to take care of them: as long as they did their jobs, they were guaranteed employment, and as long as they performed well, they could expect to be promoted. No more! With the downsizing of the early '90s, many layers of management were trimmed, and now there are fewer opportunities for promotion. To stay prepared for such changes, employees need to up-to-date, transferable skills, and they have to be ready to move into new positions as their organizations change. They also need to understand their organizations and how to navigate them. In other words, they need to be self-reliant in their careers.

Mentors and networks can help you thrive, not just survive, in today's organization. Your mentor aids you in understanding your organization, gaining skills, and preparing yourself for career moves. Your network can help you land your next job. Employees who take charge of their careers are those who initiate the search for *multiple* mentors and contacts and secure their help.

This book shows you how to locate and keep mentors who will support you. It shows you how to identify potential mentors, where to find them, how to approach them, and what to say in asking for their help. It also tells you how to start a mentoring relationship and keep it going.

In addition to having mentors, people who are self-reliant in their careers build and maintain strong networks to help them get their work done, find clients, or find new jobs. Therefore, this book also emphasizes the importance of networking. It helps you plan your networking strategy and feel more comfortable initiating a conversation, asking for help, and following up. It also stresses the importance of keeping in touch with your contacts and giving back in order to keep your network strong.

You may work in a corporation, in government, or in education, or you may be self-employed. Whatever your circumstances, the concepts in this book apply to you because the book was written for professionals in all sectors of the workforce, especially for those who want to achieve their career goals and get ahead more quickly. The concepts and steps outlined in the book are even more crucial to women and people of color, since they are so often excluded from the old boys' network. Networking and mentoring tend to occur more easily for white males, a relatively small segment of the workforce, and it's critical that others learn networking skills so they can have the same advantages.

As a small-business owner, I know the importance of networking. I don't even advertise my speaking, training, and consulting services; I rely on networking alone to get new business. As a mentoring program manager for Hewlett-Packard, I had the opportunity to facilitate the matching process for hundreds of mentors and what I call *mentees* (a term I prefer to *protégés*). I have also trained hundreds of mentors and mentees at Hewlett-Packard and at many other organizations in industry and government. In helping prospective mentees find suitable mentors, I've seen what makes a mentoring partnership successful. I also have personal experience both as a mentor and as a mentee. Here are some key questions, based on my experience, that prospective mentees ask:

- How do I find a mentor?
- What should I look for in a mentor?
- How do I ask a mentor for help, and what if he or she turns me down?
- Once I have a mentor, how do we get started?
- How do I keep the relationship going?
- What happens if the arrangement doesn't work out?

And here are a few similar questions that professionals ask about networking:

- How do I initiate a conversation?
- How should I introduce myself?
- What do I say after we introduce ourselves?
- How can I ask for help?
- How do I follow up?

These questions and more are answered in this book. You'll learn how to find and approach mentors and networking contacts, build and maintain relationships, and overcome challenges. You'll find practical, useful ideas and tips that you can implement tomorrow, and you'll be shown how to take the most important steps:

- Creating a mission statement for your business or career
- Identifying your development needs and determining how others can help you meet your needs

- Finding potential mentors and contacts
- Approaching potential mentors and contacts with specific requests
- Establishing and maintaining your mentoring and networking relationships

I interviewed many businesspeople while writing the book, and their real-life stories of how mentoring networks advanced their careers can help you learn from their successes. Many people lack confidence and feel awkward asking another person to be a mentor. My hope is that this book will give you not just the knowledge and tools but also the confidence to find and keep mentors who will support you and help you achieve your career goals.

ACKNOWLEDGMENTS

I am grateful for my mentors and network relationships; without them, I would not have been able to write this book. A significant mentor in particular, Linda Phillips-Jones, gave me the confidence to believe in myself and helped me achieve my dreams. She gave me opportunities, and she "stretched" me to do things that I wasn't sure I could do. She helped me believe that I could be a successful speaker, trainer, consultant, and author.

I am also very grateful for those people who took the time to review my book and give me honest feedback. Many thanks go to Linda Davidson, Bob McCafferty, and Jim Robinson. Their comments helped make the text clearer and more meaningful.

I especially want to thank Connie Neal, the author of more than thirty books. Connie's wisdom and expertise were invaluable. I thank her for sharing numerous tips, techniques, and advice in all phases of this book project.

In addition, I want to thank the many people who took the time to share their stories and real-life experiences with mentoring and networking relationships and helped make this book come alive: Chip Bell, Dan Berg, David Bradley, Ken Coleman, June Davidson, Janet Drez, Sally Donahe, Carlene Ellis, BB Hill, Linda Hoffman, Roz Hudnell, Van Johnson, Joe Kilkenny, Chip Koehler, Ann Livermore, Bob McCafferty, George Morrisey, Terry Paulson, the late Santiago Rodriguez, Linda Roth, Heather Shea, Donna Shirley, Betty Sproule, and Becca Williams.

Finally, I am thankful for my family, whose support and encouragement have kept me going. I am especially grateful to my two children, Kristen and Kyle, who constantly remind me of the important things in life. They've had to put up with Mom working at the computer much of the time. They've helped me maintain the right perspective and a balance of work and play throughout the project.

ABOUT THE AUTHOR

Kathleen Barton holds a bachelor's degree in psychology from Chico State University and a master's degree in business from San Jose State University, and has more than fifteen years' experience in the training and development field, primarily in management development. She held a variety of positions at Hewlett-Packard, where she worked as a training manager, a corporate trainer, a program manager, and an education consultant. She also managed an award-winning mentoring program at Hewlett-Packard for nearly five years.

A professional speaker, trainer, and consultant specializing in personal mission, mentoring/networking, and work/life balance, Barton helps organizations increase the contributions and loyalty of their employees by helping employees find purpose, meaning, and balance in their work and in the rest of their lives. As a senior consultant with The Mentoring Group, she also works with organizations to develop and retain employees through mentoring initiatives. Her clients include the California Department of Transportation, Farmers Insurance, PricewaterhouseCoopers, Space Systems/Loral, and the U.S. De-partment of Agriculture's Natural Resources Conservation Service, among others.

She served as executive producer of the videotape *Mentoring That Makes a Difference,* which has been used by companies nationwide. She is also the author of the booklet *Creating Your Personal Mission in Life* and the audiotape and workbook *The Balancing Act: Managing Work & Life.*

Kathleen Barton has been featured in *HR News,* the *Sacramento Bee,* and *Training* magazine. She is a member of the National Speakers Association, the American Society for Training and Development, and the Society for Human Resource Management. She lives with her husband, Michael, and her two children, Kristen and Kyle, in Roseville, California, and can be reached at Kathleen Barton & Associates, 1424 Southwood Way, Roseville, CA 95747 (phone: 916/789-7353; fax: 916/784-8379; e-mail: kathleen_barton@surewest.net).

CHAPTER 1

UNDERSTANDING MENTORING & NETWORKING

As shown in the following examples, mentoring and networking can open doors to new opportunities.

HEATHER SHEA

"Mentoring has made a tremendous difference in my career," says Heather Shea, coauthor with Chip Bell of *Dance Lessons: Six Steps to Great Partnerships in Business and Life* and well-known consultant and speaker. "My career has relied heavily on mentors, including Chip Bell and Tom Peters."

Heather got her start as an entry-level salesperson with the Tom Peters Group, now tompeters!company. In her first year, she broke all the sales records. Two years later, she became president. Tom Peters recognized her accomplishments and became a "big fan" of hers. As her mentor, he was very supportive. He even went on sales calls with Heather. Peters's encouragement gave her the confidence and competence to take on the role of president and COO of the firm.

After working many years as a nurse, BB Hill, principal consultant at Organization Development Associates, was ready for a career change. She went back to school to pursue a master's degree in human resource management and development, and she got involved in the American Society for Training and Development (ASTD).

As special events coordinator for ASTD, BB met and got to know a woman named Laurie, a training manager who worked on her committee. Months later the two reconnected, and Laurie told BB that she was moving to the East Coast. After asking if BB had finished the work toward her master's degree, she asked if BB would be interested in taking over her job. BB was thrilled.

In glowing terms, Laurie told her boss about BB, and BB landed the job, having been chosen over two other candidates to become training manager for a start-up training department. "I jumped from being a nurse to being a training manager," BB says today. "I never could have dreamed that would happen."

Both of these anecdotes involve people helping people. In the first, a mentor helped Heather get a promotion. In the second, a networking contact helped BB make a career change.

As Heather's story illustrates, having good mentors can enhance your career success. Linda Phillips-Jones, author of *The Mentee's Guide* and an expert on mentoring, says that finding and making use of the right mentors is the most critical step you'll ever take in your career. I couldn't agree more. A mentor can help you learn the ropes of a profession, business, or organization and help you avoid mistakes. Because a mentor has "been there and done that," he or she can make your learning curve less steep and accelerate your development.

Networking, like mentoring, can help you be successful in your business or career. According to Harvey MacKay, author of *Dig Your Well Before You're Thirsty,* "The single characteristic shared by all the truly successful people I've met over a lifetime . . . is the ability to create and nurture a network of contacts." Whether you're in sales, an entrepreneurial setting, or the corporate world, networking can benefit you. Your networking contacts can help you find a job, get promoted, get your job done more quickly, gain new customers, and get referrals.

Have you had mentors? Do you want one? Do you have a strong network of contacts who have provided valuable information? Do you want to build such a network? This book will show you how to build a network of mentoring contacts. You'll learn how to be proactive and plan your strategy, how to find and approach mentors and networking contacts, how to secure their help, how to build and maintain the mentoring relationship, and much more. But first, let's define the terms *mentoring* and *networking* and discuss the value of each strategy.

WHAT IS MENTORING?

In its simplest form, mentoring is people helping people. More specifically, mentoring is a helping relationship in which a more experienced person invests time and energy to assist the professional growth and development of another person. It is a helping relationship, and it is developmental in nature.

Notice the focus on professional development in this definition. People can have mentors in any and all areas of their lives: family, career, health and fitness, finances. There can be emotional and spiritual mentors as well. In fact, I would encourage you to have multiple mentors for the various aspects of your life. The focus of this book, however, is professional and career development.

Mentoring can be formal or informal. Formal mentoring is typically part of a program in which a mentor and a mentee are paired. (I prefer the term *mentee* to *protégé* because it connotes a role more active than the one associated with being a protégé.) Formal programs provide some kind of structure: training for mentors and mentees, mentor/mentee agreements, goals and development plans, set time frames, evaluation processes, and the like. The purposes of such programs vary from integrating new employees into an organization to succession planning for developing future leaders. Such companies as Hewlett-Packard, Kimberly-Clark, Lucent Technologies, and PricewaterhouseCoopers have formal mentoring programs.

The focus of this book is informal mentoring relationships. Informal mentoring is more casual and unstructured. It takes place more naturally. The mentor and mentee come together on their own. They may meet at work, through a professional organization, or by some other means. Often they have contact with each other through a project, a team, a professional organization, or a volunteer effort. They see value in developing a relationship: the mentor sees potential in the mentee, and this vision sparks the relationship, or the mentee realizes that he or she can learn something of value from the mentor. In these cases, the term *mentor* may not even be used. The mentor—the more experienced person—provides help to the other person. The two may meet on a spontaneous or occasional basis. Mentoring may be an off-the-cuff arrangement whereby the mentee gets in touch with the mentor as necessary for direction and guidance. Or the two may meet on a regular basis—for example, to have lunch once a month. They may communicate by phone, by e-mail, or face to face.

Some mentoring relationships last for years. For example, George Morrisey, a business consultant and author, has been a mentor for more than fifteen years to Terry Paulson, a psychologist and author. In other mentoring relationships, which may be as brief as a few interactions, people come and go, providing help when it is most needed. For example, Linda Hoffman, managing partner at PricewaterhouseCoopers, got involved in the organization Women in Business, where she came to know a succession of role models and mentors.

Now that you have a good understanding of mentoring, let's expand our definitions of the terms *mentor* and *mentee*. According to Linda Phillips-Jones, a mentor is any experienced person who goes out of his or her way to help another person reach important goals:

- The mentor is more experienced than the mentee. The mentor isn't necessarily older, just more experienced in some way.
- The mentor goes out of his or her way to help. This is what differentiates a mentor from a role model. A role model is someone whom you look up to, admire, and aspire to be like. But unless that person goes out of the way to help, he or she is not a mentor.
- The relationship is goal oriented. It is focused on the mentee's development or career goals.

A mentee, by contrast, according to Gordon Shea, author of *Making the Most of Being Mentored,* is the recipient of a mentor's help, especially if the mentee has sought this help and uses it for developmental purposes:

- The mentee is an active participant in the process, not just a sponge soaking up information from the mentor.
- The mentee should be *proactive.* He or she is someone who knows his or her development needs and seeks help in those areas.

BENEFITS OF MENTORING

"So," you may be asking, "what's in it for me?"

FOR MENTEES

As a mentee, you can benefit greatly from a mentoring relationship. Here is what you can gain:

- Knowledge and skills
- Coaching, advice, guidance, and support
- An understanding of organizational culture and politics
- New opportunities and contacts
- Greater career success

KNOWLEDGE AND SKILLS You can gain new knowledge and skills from mentors. Heather Shea learned leadership skills from Tom Peters. She also learned about speaking and writing—and even a little bit about baseball! As a mentee, you can learn a lot more quickly than you might otherwise because you can learn firsthand from an expert and can also learn from his or her mistakes. Therefore, you can avoid trial-and-error mistakes.

COACHING, ADVICE, GUIDANCE, AND SUPPORT I like to think of having a mentor as having your own personal coach. Your mentor is someone you can go to for information, idea testing, and advice. “I know I can go to George for assistance anytime,” says Terry Paulson of his mentor, George Morrisey. We all need that kind of support. A mentor’s coaching and advice can help you make better decisions and get better results!

UNDERSTANDING OF ORGANIZATIONAL CULTURE AND POLITICS A mentor can give you insight into organizational culture. You can learn appropriate behavior and protocol. A mentor can even teach you the unwritten rules. A mentor can teach you how to get things done within the organizational framework. For someone new to an organization, this is invaluable and can save time and frustration.

When Carlene Ellis was hired as director of planning and control at Intel, she was one of the two highest-level women in the company. She buddied up with Cindy Burgdorf, the controller. “I learned the politics and culture of the organization,” says Carlene. “Cindy was a major contributor to my adjustment to a new company and new job.”

NEW OPPORTUNITIES AND CONTACTS A mentor can open doors for you by providing new opportunities (for example, to attend an important meeting, give a presentation, or take on a new and challenging assignment). Your mentor may also introduce you to new contacts—people who are able to advance your career or who are potential clients.

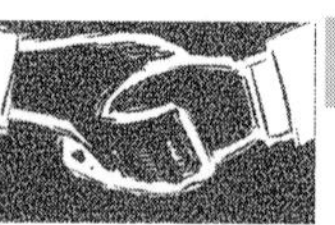

DAVID BRADLEY Currently a physicist at Lawrence Livermore National Laboratories, David Bradley shares how his mentor, Joe Kilkenny, gave him opportunities early in his career. “After I completed my Ph.D., Joe invited me to go to Livermore to do a laser experiment. This project helped my visibility."

It also opened up an opportunity for David to contract with the lab to do laser experiments. Soon thereafter, the project owner retired. “Joe encouraged them to give me a permanent job,” David says. “He said I was the ideal person to do it.” As a result, David was offered the job.

GREATER CAREER SUCCESS Ultimately, the benefits just described result in greater career success. That's what happened for Carlene Ellis, whom we just met.

As a result of help from her mentor, Carlene Ellis was promoted to the position of manager of computer operations at Fairchild Instruments.

Burleigh Cook, head of information systems, thought Carlene had potential. He was impressed with her, particularly when, after her first month on the job, she stood up in a project-review meeting for what she believed was right, despite opposition.

An opening came up in Burleigh's department, and he told the CEO he wanted to put Carlene in the job.

"She's 30 years old," the CEO said, "and she's a girl."

Burleigh replied, "She's the best guy on my staff."

Carlene got the job—an almost unheard-of three-level promotion. "Burleigh gave me a chance to prove myself," says Carlene. And prove herself she did! Carlene later worked for Burleigh in two other management positions.

FOR MENTORS

Mentors also benefit from a mentoring relationship, sometimes as much as or even more than mentees.

"I feel like I've derived the greater benefit," says Chip Bell, author of *Managers as Mentors.* "I feel in debt because I get so much out of it."

What do mentors gain?

- Learning and a broader perspective
- Validation and reinforcement
- Personal satisfaction

LEARNING AND A BROADER PERSPECTIVE Mentees learn from mentors, and mentors learn from mentees. For example, mentors can learn about the perceptions and the unique challenges of others in the organization. This is valuable information that they might not otherwise gain.

VALIDATION AND REINFORCEMENT When mentors share their knowledge, skill, and expertise, it is validating for them. "It makes me realize that I know a lot about my field," say Laura Lee Morel, market research manager at Hewlett-Packard Company. Mentors also receive the respect and admiration of their mentees. What person doesn't want to feel respected, admired, and validated? "The ego factor is part of it," George Morrisey says. "It's a compliment to be asked for help."

PERSONAL SATISFACTION By far the most commonly cited benefit I hear from mentors is simply the personal satisfaction of helping another person. Many mentors have been helped in their own careers, and they see mentoring as a way of giving back. Mentors find it very rewarding to help others learn and grow in their careers, especially when their mentees are successful.

"When my mentee is successful—an executive gets promoted, or an author's book does well—I have a sense of pride that I had a part in it," says Chip Bell.

As president of Business Customer Organization at Hewlett-Packard Com-pany, Ann Livermore has learned a great deal from various mentors in her organization. Manuel Diaz taught her how to really listen to a customer and, through questioning, move a person to a solution. Ann also learned by observing Dick Hackborn and Marc Hoff. "Dick was the best business strategist, and Marc was operationally savvy" says Ann.

But Ann's most significant mentor was Jim Arthur, from whom she learned a lot about how to run an operation. A few key insights have stayed with her, and she practices these principles today. First, Jim taught her about priorities. "Ann, you care about too many things," he would say. "Ten years from now, will it really matter?" Ann learned that she had to care about the right things. In her role as president, she understands that she can't do it all.

Second, Jim taught Ann to choose her battles—to focus on what makes sense and what is most important.

Third, Jim taught Ann the importance of picking out the most important points in a conversation. "What are the three takeaways?" he would ask.

Ann's ability to set priorities and to focus has helped her be successful. The knowledge, skills, and experience she gained from her mentors have been invaluable and have contributed to her success as a leader in the company.

WHAT IS NETWORKING?

The term *networking* is relatively new, but networking itself has been around forever. The term is used to denote the age-old practice of building relationships. More specifically, networking is a lifelong process of meeting people, making contacts, and building mutually beneficial professional relationships.

Networking is often misunderstood. Networking is not selling. It is about making contacts, getting to know people, and developing relationships. It is about wanting to help people who also want to help you (see Table 1, on the next page).

Networking links people with information. It involves gathering and disseminating information, being a resource for others, and calling on people for help. Networking, then, is not just about receiving; it is also about giving. Both parties benefit from a networking interaction. Networking is underscored by the power of cooperation.

NETWORKING AND MENTORING

How is networking related to mentoring? Networking and mentoring are very similar but not the same. Mentoring is a special type of networking relationship in which a more skilled or experienced person helps another reach professional goals. By definition, the mentee receives most of the help, although the mentor also benefits. Mentoring is a two-way relationship. It involves regular contact and is focused on goals. It is generally, but not always, a longer-term relationship than most networking relationships.

TABLE 1 What Networking Is . . . and Is Not

Networking Is . . .	Networking Is Not . . .
Making contacts	Selling
Getting to know people and developing relationships	Being impersonal
Promoting something of value	Impressing others
Asking assertively and offering graciously	Manipulation
Exchanging business cards when there is a reason to stay in touch	Passing out business cards for no particular reason
Giving with no expectations	Keeping score
Serving people	Using people
A way of life	A technique

Beverly Kaye, author of the article "Shared Brain Power," coined the term *mentworking* to describe "a process of giving and receiving by participating in relationships in which everyone is a learner and a teacher." The idea is to create a learning network of professional contacts to help you accomplish your goals and help others accomplish theirs. For career success, everyone should be involved simultaneously in mentoring and networking relationships.

BENEFITS OF NETWORKING

Why network? The old adage "It's not what you know but who you know" is definitely true. Networking opens doors to opportunities, whether you're job hunting, in business as an entrepreneur, or working in the corporate world.

CAREER FOCUS If you are job hunting, your contacts can help you find your ideal job. According to Lillian Bjorseth, author of *Breakthrough*

Networking, at least 85 percent of all jobs are found through referrals. Rather than spend your time wading through the want ads, try connecting with people who work in organizations that you want to work for.

Dan Berg is deputy program manager at Space Systems/Loral. When Dan graduated from college, a friend of the family, Ralph, opened a door for him. Ralph had spent forty years in the aerospace business. "He made one phone call," Dan recalls, "and told me I had an interview with Ford Aerospace. I interviewed with eight different people and had five offers. I accepted an offer as an associate engineer."

Networking is important at all stages of your career. It provides you with career security—not necessarily job security, but career security. If you find your job in jeopardy, your support system of contacts can help you find a position in another part of your organization or a job outside the organization. With job security a thing of the past, you need a support network as a safety net. And not only can your network help you find another job; it can help you get promoted. If influential people in the organization speak highly of you, others are more likely to be receptive to you and your work.

Sally Donahe was the first female master sergeant in the Massachusetts National Guard. "Lieutenant Colonel Elisabeth Robinson was instrumental in my promotion," Sally says. "She had the ear of senior leadership. She spoke highly of me and touted my accomplishments."

Another way networking can help you in your career is by helping you improve your performance. Research by Robert Kelley, author of *How to Be a Star at Work,* indicates that networking is one of the key strategies used by star performers in organizations. Networking helps employees by putting them in contact with valuable people and information. High-performing employees are able to turn to their networks and quickly gather the information they need to solve problems.

"Networking has increased my work productivity," says Betty Sproule, marketing manager at Hewlett-Packard Company. Betty is a top performer and was selected for a high-potential leadership development program. "Through my connection of contacts," she says, "I'm able to get more done in a shorter time. I know who to go to for information." Effective networkers are able to get much more accomplished than people who spend lots of time gathering information and investigating solutions.

BUSINESS FOCUS If you are in business for yourself or are in sales, networking is an invaluable marketing and sales tool. According to Lillian Bjorseth, more than 50 percent of all businesses fail within the first seven years of their existence. Networking provides some insurance to help you stay in business.

The most cost-effective marketing activity is word-of-mouth advertising. This is where networking comes into play. By networking, you can build your own personal sales force. When you connect with other people, and when you help each other out, you multiply your resources. Having a network of people helping you market your business is a lot easier than going it alone. Word-of-mouth marketing works: it's a lot more effective to have others say good things about you and your products and services than to say such things yourself.

Networking helps entrepreneurs and sales representatives build strong client relationships. It can help you create new business, get referral business, and gain repeat business. The secret is networking contacts. The fact is, people want to do business with people they know, like, and trust.

There's a big difference between a cold call and a warm call. A warm call is a call to someone you know through one of your contacts. Someone has recommended you, and the mutual relationship softens the sales call. A hot call is even more beneficial. A hot call is a call made with a strong recommendation and an obvious fit. For example, I recently gained new business that originated from a hot call. A fellow consultant had recommended me to a colleague of hers. "You need to talk to Kathleen," she said. "Kathleen's an expert in mentoring." Contacts get you in the door. They give you the opportunity to be heard. But once you're in, you need to sell yourself on the basis of your expertise and credibility.

It's a tough market. We need all the help we can get, and networking helps you get ahead of your competition. It's always useful to know what your competitors are doing. If you're well connected, your networking contacts can provide valuable information. If you can learn from your contacts what your competitors are up to, you can stay one step ahead.

Becca Williams, an entrepreneur, took the networking concept to the next level and formed a networking group. Becca's story illustrates the power of networking and collaboration.

BECCA WILLIAMS

Last spring, six women business owners, including myself, formed an online group to share information and offer one another support. The group has been extremely beneficial to everyone involved. We've acted as mentors to one another in our areas of expertise and shared contact lists, information on generating PR, creating media kits and other marketing tactics, Web design and HTML knowledge, and advice on time management. A few of us have even swapped services, such as graphic design, Web design and maintenance, and advertising space. All of this sharing was great, but we finally met in person in October, and the story gets even better!

Four of us held a "meeting of the minds" at a vacation home to brainstorm ideas for one another's businesses and offer further assistance in bringing those ideas to reality. The end result of the meeting was the formation of a new company. One woman's Web site had reached a point where a single person could no longer handle all aspects of running the company, and the business had a lot of unrealized potential. We saw that the combination of our skill sets and interests formed a solid basis for a company and that our individual contacts would help us round out the rest of the management team and board of advisors.

We are a three-hour drive apart, but we communicate daily via telephone and e-mail and meet in person once a month. We're in the process of redoing some of the technical aspects of the Web site and plan to expand the concept to a network of related sites. The business plan is being written, several advisors have agreed to sit on our board, and soon we'll start looking for investors. It's an incredible networking experience, and I feel very fortunate to have found my way into such an active, successful group of women!

THE IMPORTANCE OF MENTORING AND NETWORKING FOR SPECIAL GROUPS

We've been talking about the value of mentoring and networking. These strategies are even more important to certain groups of people: those, particularly women and people of color, who face special challenges or obstacles in the workplace. These groups are typically excluded from the old boys' network.

Mentoring occurs more naturally for white men. They gain insider information, learn appropriate protocol, and become politically savvy. Because women and people of color do not receive the benefits of this informal network, they need to seek mentoring and help on their own in order to gain the same benefits. They need to be proactive and initiate relationships. This can be particularly challenging for some people, especially women, who are not taught how to ask for help. They are socialized to be caregivers and nurturers, and so they often feel more comfortable giving help to others than asking for it. But this is a challenge that has to be met, and it is addressed in Chapter Five, "Approaching Mentors and Contacts."

Women and people of color are more likely to be isolated in executive management positions, where all or most of their colleagues tend to be white men. Women find themselves in the minority in such traditionally male-dominated fields as aerospace and civil or mechanical engineering. They need role models and guides, and they need to know how to find them. They need assistance with handling these special challenges. Remember Carlene Ellis? She's a case in point.

CARLENE ELLIS

When Carlene Ellis was in college, back in the 1960s, there were very few women pursuing degrees in math or science. One of Carlene's early mentors was her math teacher, Professor Johnson. He encouraged Carlene, whereas other professors discouraged her. (One even asked her why she didn't just take home economics. "I'd flunk," Carlene told him.) Professor Johnson gave her courage. "He was crucial to my finishing my mathematics degree," Carlene recalls. "Otherwise, I might have dropped out." She persevered and became one of a few women to complete a math degree at the University of Georgia.

SANTIAGO RODRIGUEZ

The late Santiago Rodriguez, who was director of diversity at Microsoft Corporation, had a number of mentors over the course of his career. His first mentor was Mr. Szolt, his seventh-grade teacher, who was Hungarian. "He identified with me and took me under his wing," said Santiago. "He sat me down every week to learn English. He created in me a thirst for knowledge."

Santiago's first job after graduate school was in the Office of the Secretary of the Air Force as a writer and editor. "My mentor, Harry Zubkoff, taught me a love of writing. If you know how to write, speak, and get along with people, that's 90 percent of being successful."

Others were also influential in Santiago's career. William H. Brown III, chairman of the Equal Employment Opportunity Commission, was a "tremendous influence"; his experience working with William Brown led Santiago to his work at Microsoft. He learned how to deal with delicate and confidential issues, and how to get things done without formal power. He also learned how to initiate a program and implement change.

Other mentors gave him new opportunities and broadened his vistas: President Donald Kennedy of Stanford University, for example, and Kevin Sullivan, senior vice president of human resources at Apple Computer. Kennedy taught Santiago how to communicate effectively, and Sullivan taught him how to think strategically and how to become a business partner.

These mentoring experiences gave Santiago valued knowledge, skills, and experience. "My mentors taught me that an individual can make a difference," Santiago said.

SUMMARY

- Finding good mentors and learning from them is the most crucial step you can take in your career. Truly successful people create and nurture networks of contacts.
- Mentoring is a helping relationship in which a more experienced person invests time and energy in contributing to the professional growth and development of another person.
- A mentor is any experienced person who goes out of his or her way to help another person reach important goals. A mentee is the beneficiary of a mentor's help, especially one who seeks out this help and uses it appropriately for developmental purposes.
- A mentee benefits from mentoring by gaining knowledge and skills; receiving coaching, advice, guidance, and support; gaining an understanding of organizational culture and politics; and obtaining new opportunities and contacts. These factors lead to greater career success.
- Mentees and mentors alike benefit from the mentoring relationship. Mentors gain a broader perspective, receive validation, and feel personal satisfaction.
- Networking is a lifelong process of meeting people, making contacts, and building mutually beneficial professional relationships.
- Networking can help you find a job, get promoted, get your job done more quickly, gain new customers, get referrals and repeat business, and get ahead of the competition.
- Mentoring and networking are even more important to women, people of color, and others who face special challenges or obstacles.

LEARNING TOOLS

1. Analyze your past mentoring and networking experiences, using Worksheet 1. Think of a past mentor who had a significant impact on you. (Maybe you didn't even call this person a mentor.) Was there anyone who went out of his or her way to help you reach important goals? For each mentoring relationship, write down the following elements:

   - How the relationship began
   - What specific help the mentor provided
   - How you contributed to the relationship
   - How you benefited

   Then do the same for a key networking contact. Use the following example to get started.

   - How the relationship began:

     Mary was my first boss at Corning. This was my first job after college.

   - What specific help the mentor provided:

     Mary gave me feedback and pointed out my need to become more assertive. She suggested a class and some good books. She coached me on a few occasions when I was facing difficult interactions.

   - How I contributed to the relationship:

     I received the feedback without defensiveness. I followed through by taking a class and reading a book. I initiated a conversation about an issue that I was facing, and I asked for her help.

   - How I benefited:

     I gained new skills in assertiveness. I increased my confidence. I am able to confront others more confidently and state what I want.

WORKSHEET 1 Mentoring History

	Mentor	Networking Contact
How the relationship began		
Specific help provided		
How I contributed		
How I benefited		

Analyzing each relationship will help you understand not only what you got out of it but also what you put into it. There may be things you are already doing, without realizing it, to establish and maintain mentoring and networking relationships. (In the chapters to come, we'll discuss your role in finding and approaching mentors and contacts and in establishing and maintaining mentoring and networking relationships.)

2. List three to five specific reasons why you personally can benefit from a mentor's help. Then list three to five specific reasons why you personally can benefit from having a strong network (see Worksheet 2).

3. Now circle the most compelling reason on each of your two lists. Keep these reasons in mind as you read the rest of this book. If you focus on the potential benefits, you will stay motivated not just to keep reading but also to take action and apply these concepts to your career.

WORKSHEET 2 Benefits of Mentoring and Networking

Benefits of Having a Mentor	Benefits of Having a Strong Network

CHAPTER 2

DEVELOPING A MENTOR NETWORK

Mentoring and networking have changed over the years to adapt to the changing environment of organizations and work. With the new challenges in the work world today, professionals need to be more proactive and initiate helping relationships. They need to build mentor networks in order to succeed in the new environment.

THE CHANGING ORGANIZATION

Traditionally, an older, more experienced manager took a younger, less sophisticated person under his wing and showed him the ropes. He'd show his protégé how to succeed in the organizational culture and avoid making mistakes. The protégé then became a member of the old boys' network, which gave him access to insider information and power. The mentor would choose someone with potential—typically, someone who was like himself, who looked, thought, and acted the way he did.

As a result, this system brought about favoritism and discrimination, and it perpetuated the values and behaviors of the past.

Organizations have changed, so mentoring also has needed to change. Organizations are now flatter; they have fewer layers and are less hierarchical. Employees need to do more with less and to be more flexible. Organizations need people who can quickly learn new skill sets and adapt to change. Decision making has been pushed down to the lowest level, and decisions need to be made more quickly in the fast-changing environment. There is greater focus on the team. Diverse skills and viewpoints are needed.

The changing organization has brought about the need for *career self-reliance*. With the end of lifelong employment, employees need to take charge of their careers. They need to think the way entrepreneurs do, always keeping at the front of their minds what value they bring to the organization. Employees need to own their development and their careers, hence the concept of the proactive professional. In this changing work environment, employees need effective networks of contacts in order to gain insider information and prepare themselves for impending organizational developments. They also need mentors in order to quickly acquire the knowledge and skills that are needed for making the transition into new jobs and being successful in their new organizations. Networking and mentoring are ways to stay current professionally and keep up with what's going on in the organization.

Entrepreneurs need networks of contacts and mentors even more than people in large organizations do. Competition is fierce: 50 percent of new businesses fail. New entrepreneurs need connections with others. They need to learn from others who have been successful in their businesses. They need to learn management, marketing, finance, production—all the aspects of running a business. They need practical advice so they can avoid making mistakes that will cost them business.

You, too, need to take responsibility for your career or business and *own* your development. That's what proactive professionals do. What do proactive mentees and networkers look like?

THE PROACTIVE MENTEE

Today's proactive mentees initiate mentoring relationships and acquire multiple mentors. They are very focused on their development and career goals, and they actively manage the mentoring relationship.

PROACTIVE MENTEES INITIATE MENTORING RELATIONSHIPS

In the past, mentors did the choosing. Now mentees are initiating relationships. They are seeking out people who are successful in their careers, mentors whose backgrounds, skills, and experience match their own development needs. "I've always been very proactive about making contact with people I could learn from," says Linda Hoffman, managing partner of PricewaterhouseCoopers. "When I meet someone I can learn from, I build a relationship. We go have lunch and talk."

PROACTIVE MENTEES SEEK MULTIPLE MENTORING RELATIONSHIPS

Mentees today are seeking multiple mentors for different goals and different developmental needs. Nevertheless, many people are still looking for that one "nirvana" mentor, the one who can meet every need. But that person doesn't exist. You can't expect one person to provide everything. Instead, you should build a network of mentors from whom you can learn. "It's important to have mentoring relationships with a number of people," says Linda Hoffman. This strategy has paid off in Linda's career: she was one of the youngest people ever to be promoted to partner in her firm.

PROACTIVE MENTEES FOCUS ON THEIR GOALS

Mentees today set development and career goals, and mentoring is focused on those goals, with an emphasis on specific things that mentees can do to reach them. Therefore, mentoring relationships are generally very practical and focused on learning that can be applied right away. The time frame for mentoring is also shorter than in the past, and mentoring relationships last months rather than years. This change is driven by the fast-paced work environment and the need for immediate results.

PROACTIVE MENTEES MANAGE THE RELATIONSHIP

Proactive mentees are active participants in the mentoring process. In fact, they drive the relationship from beginning to end. After all, it is their development, and so they want to get their needs met. They ask questions and seek specific assistance. They also track their progress and determine what they need next. It's important to realize that you get out of the mentoring relationship what you put into it.

ASSESS YOURSELF AS A PROACTIVE MENTEE

Are you ready for the challenge? Do you have what it takes to become a proactive mentee? You need to be ready to enter into a mentoring relationship. According to Carlene Ellis, whom we met in the last chapter, "the mere acquisition of a mentor will not help unless you're ready to be mentored." Successful mentees have a number of characteristics. (You'll have an opportunity to assess your readiness as a proactive mentee at the end of this chapter.)

- *Proactive mentees are clear about their goals.* They have career goals and clearly defined developmental goals to help them reach their career goals. And they are able to clearly communicate their goals to their mentors.
- *Proactive mentees are assertive.* They aren't afraid to initiate mentoring relationships and ask for the help they need. They are active participants in the mentoring partnership.
- *Proactive mentees are willing to accept a mentor's help.* They are willing to trust and open up, and to take direction.

- *Proactive mentees are good listeners.* They listen with open minds and are willing to try out new ideas. They listen attentively and ask questions to clarify what was said.
- *Proactive mentees can accept constructive feedback.* They are not threatened by feedback; instead, they see it as a gift. They value feedback as a learning opportunity. They are able to hear feedback, assess it objectively, and determine what actions they need to take. They listen nondefensively to their mentors' advice.
- *Proactive mentees follow through on commitments.* They can be counted on to do what they say they will do. They follow through by returning phone calls, showing up for meetings, completing assignments, and so forth.
- *Proactive mentees show appreciation toward their mentors.* They are good about thanking their mentors. They show appreciation through their words or by sending notes or small gifts. They are also able to share credit with their mentors for accomplishments and give back to their mentors by offering help.
- *Proactive mentees are self-confident.* They believe in their own abilities and are willing to admit their weaknesses. Their confidence allows them to ask for help, accept feedback, and share credit.

THE PROACTIVE NETWORKER

In Chapter One, we learned the value of networking. We learned that truly successful people create and nurture a network of contacts. A network can help you advance in your career or build your business.

In networking, just as in mentoring, the key to success is being proactive. Proactive professionals know that they are in charge of their careers. They value networking and mentoring as their most important tools for career management. They know the importance of building a lifetime support system.

What do proactive networkers look like? They network in a way that is natural, effective, and mutually beneficial. They have six key characteristics.

- *Proactive networkers are prepared to network.* They know their goals. They know their businesses or organizations and the value that they bring to them. They know how to effectively introduce themselves. They do their homework and prepare for networking events. They carry their business cards with them wherever they go. Therefore, they are prepared to take advantage of opportunities. There's a lot of truth to the saying "Luck is preparation meeting opportunity."
- *Proactive networkers make networking a priority.* They understand the importance of building a lifelong network. They realize the benefits to themselves, and so they carve out the time to network on a consistent basis. Rather than waiting until times of need, they network during up times and down. When they need their networks, their networks are there to support them.
- *Proactive networkers are assertive and self-confident.* They can walk confidently into a room in which they know no one. They know how to approach people and initiate conversation with ease. They feel comfortable exchanging business cards, and they are able to ask for help when they need it.
- *Proactive networkers are supportive of others.* They are genuinely interested in other people. They ask questions to learn more about others. They listen intently, without interrupting. In fact, they listen more than they talk. They are responsive and eager to help. Proactive networkers look for opportunities to offer help to others.
- *Proactive networkers treat people respectfully and graciously.* They make everyone they meet feel important.
- *Proactive networkers are professional.* Above all, they are people of integrity who "walk their talk." They do what they say they are going to do. They follow through on promises. If they say they will follow up and send you information, they do it.

Proactive networkers encounter many more opportunities than other people do; it almost seems as if opportunities miraculously come up wherever they go. This is because they have mastered the art of networking. The six characteristics just described contribute to successful networking, and you will have the opportunity to assess yourself on them at the end of this chapter.

Networking has contributed significantly to the career of Donna Shirley, assistant dean of engineering at the University of Oklahoma and former program manager for the Mars Exploration Project at Jet Propulsion Labs. Donna is involved in myriad organizations. Her contacts have brought about numerous opportunities.

One such opportunity led to two more. Donna was on the board of trustees of Scripps College, where her daughter was enrolled, and Donna was asked to give the commencement address. The president of Harvey Mudd College learned from someone who heard Donna's address that she had done a fabulous job, and he asked Donna to give the commencement address at Harvey Mudd. With that connection, Donna met the dean of social sciences, who in turn asked her to review the social sciences curriculum.

OPPORTUNITIES ABOUND

Opportunities to network are all around. You can network at almost any time and in almost any place; you never know when and where an opportunity may arise. Here are the most opportune times to network:

- *When you're facing a business challenge:* starting a new business, building a business, expanding your business to another location, hiring, looking for a new vendor or supplier
- *When you're facing career challenges:* looking for a new job opportunity, making a career change, investigating different careers
- *When you're looking for ideas or information:* wanting to brainstorm, seeking information to solve a problem, wanting feedback on your plans

With whom do you network? Almost anyone. You can network with people in your office or professional organization or even with someone you meet at the grocery store. Here are some important people to network with:

- *Professional contacts:* colleagues, peers, potential clients, business prospects

- *Organization members:* people who belong to professional organizations, community or civic organizations, volunteer organizations, churches

- *Personal contacts*: friends, family members, neighbors

It's important to diversify your network. Most people associate with people who are like them, but this is limiting. If we interact only with people who look, think, and act the way we do, then we will not be exposed to new ideas and viewpoints; we will not be stretching ourselves. You need to build a network of people from different backgrounds, fields of expertise, cultures, religions, and so on. Doing so will expose you to a rich diversity of thinking, styles, approaches, and ideas. By gaining a broader perspective, you can make better decisions and come up with more creative solutions.

ROZ HUDNELL As worldwide community education manager at Intel, Roz Hudnell relies on a strong and diverse network to get her job done. "Networking has given me an incredible database to pull from," Roz says. "It's given me the opportunity to share and listen, to grow and think more broadly. I can test ideas on people and get feedback."

When Roz was vice president of the Urban League in Sacramento, California, she created a successful training center to help people in the community gain job skills. "I had a breadth and depth of people to pull from in designing a successful center," she reports.

Where can you network? Almost anywhere: at a business conference or on a golf course, in a restaurant or on a plane, in the dentist's office or at your child's soccer game. For example, I was at the airport in Seattle, waiting for a flight, when it was announced that my flight would be delayed by an hour. Anxious to get home, I was disappointed by the delay and was considering how best to spend the time when a man next to me, a social services representative, struck up a very interesting conversation with me. He was intrigued by my areas of specialty and asked me to send him information on work/life balance. We've kept in touch since then, and he has referred me to a few potential clients. Here are some likely settings for networking:

- *Business events:* meetings, conferences, conventions, trade shows
- *Organizational functions:* meetings and other gatherings of alumni, industry associations, professional organizations, civic organizations, philanthropic organizations
- *Clubs:* social, hobbyist, and health clubs

The list could go on and on. Wherever you are, be on the lookout for opportunities to meet people. You never know who will cross your path and how the relationship may develop.

MAKE NETWORKING AND MENTORING A PART OF YOUR LIFE

Proactive professionals have made networking and mentoring a part of their lives, and through practice it's a part that comes naturally. You may be thinking that you're not outgoing or comfortable meeting new people, but you don't need to be outgoing to be an effective networker. Introverts make some of the best networkers because they listen so well.

Anyone can learn to be a proactive networker or mentee. Like swinging a golf club or strumming a guitar, networking and mentoring are skills that can be learned. Just like any other skill, networking and mentoring take practice, patience, and persistence. To gain knowledge and skills in the areas of networking and mentoring, you need the desire to learn and an attitude conducive to learning.

Because the focus is on mutually beneficial relationships, you should be focused, when it comes to networking, on helping others and looking for opportunities to assist others who may be able to help you. When it comes to mentoring, you need to think about ways to give back to your mentor.

When you have the right attitude, you are always on the lookout for opportunities to learn. When you meet people you might ask yourself, "How can I learn from this person? What knowledge, information, expertise, or experience does she have that can benefit me?" Ann Livermore, president of Business Customer Organization at

Hewlett-Packard Company, believes that we need to be constantly learning. "Really great leaders are always learning," says Ann.

Proactive professionals keep these things foremost in their minds. They are focused on learning and helping others. With this attitude, they look for opportunities wherever they go, whatever they do, and with whomever they meet. They are interested in people, and they get to know them. They build relationships. They have made networking a part of their lives, and they have formed multiple mentoring relationships. Ken Coleman, executive vice president of global operations at Silicon Graphics, says of networking, "I don't think about it. I just do it. It's part of who I am."

The rest of this book gives you a step-by-step process for initiating and developing mentoring and networking relationships. The learning tools at the end of each chapter provide opportunities for you to practice each step. These are skills that you can apply today. Consistent practice will help you master the skills required to be a proactive mentee or networker.

SUMMARY

- The changing organization has brought about the need for career self-reliance. Proactive professionals take responsibility for their development.
- Proactive mentees initiate multiple mentoring relationships, focus on their goals, and manage their relationships.
- Successful mentees possess certain characteristics. They have clearly defined goals, are assertive, are willing to accept a mentor's help, are good listeners, accept constructive feedback, follow through with commitments, show appreciation to their mentors, and are self-confident.
- Successful networkers are prepared, committed, assertive, supportive, respectful and gracious, and, above all, professional.
- Opportunities to network are all around. You can network at almost any time and in almost any place.
- Proactive professionals have made networking and mentoring a part of their lives.
- Networking and mentoring are skills that can be learned.
- Proactive professionals have the right attitude. They focus on learning and helping others.

LEARNING TOOLS

1. Assess your potential as a mentee candidate. Complete the self-assessment in Worksheet 3.

WORKSHEET 3 Self-Assessment for Proactive Mentees

Characteristic	Almost Always	Often	Sometimes	Rarely
I have clearly defined development goals.				
I am assertive and can ask for help when I need it.				
I am willing to accept a mentor's help.				
I am a good listener.				
I can accept constructive feedback.				
I follow through on commitments.				
I show appreciation toward my mentors.				
I am self-confident.				

If you answered "Almost Always" or "Often" to all the characteristics, congratulations! You have what it takes to be a proactive mentee. If not, choose one or two areas to work on, and set a goal for each one.

2. Using Worksheet 4, check your potential as a proactive networker.

WORKSHEET 4 Self-Assessment for Proactive Networkers

Characteristic	Almost Always	Often	Sometimes	Rarely
I am prepared.				
I am committed.				
I am assertive.				
I am supportive.				
I am respectful and gracious.				
I am professional.				

If you answered "Almost Always" or "Often" to all the characteristics, congratulations! You have what it takes to be a proactive networker. If not, choose one or two areas to work on, and set a goal for each one.

CHAPTER 3

PLANNING YOUR STRATEGY

"If you don't know where you are going, then any path will take you there." This quote from Lewis Carroll's *Alice's Adventures in Wonderland* points out the need to know your direction. Before you start networking and looking for mentors, you need to know your goals.

Start with a strategy. In creating your strategy, and before you identify who can best help you, you need to define your career or business mission and goals as well as your development objectives. Once you determine your needs, you can identify who can help, and how.

Your strategy, then, will encompass the following elements:

- Your business or career mission statement
- Your business or career goal
- Your development objectives

YOUR BUSINESS OR CAREER MISSION STATEMENT

Your business or career mission statement clarifies your purpose. It defines what you offer, to whom, and why. It is a guiding statement that provides focus and direction. It should inspire you to achieve success. The process of writing a mission statement requires that you think about what you want to accomplish, for whom, and why. It clarifies the value you bring to your customers or your organization.

Your mission statement answers the questions What? Who? and Why? Your business mission statement defines your products and services, your target market, and the benefits that you provide. It includes the following elements:

- What product or service you sell
- Who your customers are
- Why your customers buy from you

Donna Fisher, in her book *People Power,* suggests that your career mission statement include statements of the following elements:

- What you do that is of value
- Who benefits from what you do
- Why you are the best person to do what you do

Here is my own business mission statement: "I help organizations increase the contributions and loyalty of their employees through speaking, training, and coaching. I do this by helping employees attain a greater sense of purpose, meaning, and balance in their work and their lives." And here are some other examples of mission statements:

- Cash Flow Solutions provides individuals and small businesses with the knowledge and skills to optimize their financial assets and gain empowerment toward financial freedom.
- My career mission is to use my expertise in knowledge management to provide the most thorough, up-to-date information to my customers in a timely manner.

Now it's your turn. Using Worksheet 5, build and write down your mission statement.

WORKSHEET 5 Creating a Mission Statement

What is the product, service, or skill that I offer?

Who benefits from it?

What is the value of what I have to offer?

My business or career mission statement:

YOUR BUSINESS OR CAREER GOAL

Once you have defined your mission statement, you are ready to set a business or career goal. Your goal flows out of your mission. Ask yourself, "To be as successful as I want to be, what do I need to do?" Maybe you need to increase your customer base or expand your business in some way. Maybe you need to attain a more senior-level position in your field. Your business or career goal identifies a specific end result to be achieved within a specific time frame. Here are some examples of goals:

- Earn $1 million in business revenues by the year 2004
- Increase my client base by 25 percent over the next two years
- Attain a management position in the next year
- Achieve the highest performance ranking in my job by year's end

I suggest that you keep the time frame short—between one and three years. Using Worksheet 6, take some time now to thoughtfully determine your goal.

WORKSHEET 6 Setting a Business or Career Goal

What do I need to do to fulfill my mission?

What specifically do I want to achieve in the next one to three years?

My business or career goal:

YOUR DEVELOPMENT OBJECTIVES

Once you've determined your goal, you're ready to identify your development objectives. What do you need to do in order to achieve your goal? If you want to increase your client base, maybe you need to focus more effort on marketing and sales. If you want to attain a management position, you need to determine the skills required of managers and identify those skills that you need to develop. Objectives that focus on skill development are most effective.

What skills do you need to develop? The mentee development assessment at the end of this chapter will help you determine your skill need. Pick one to three areas on which to focus; any more than that will be too much for you to focus on at once. Then write development objectives, such as (1) develop project management skills, (2) develop leadership skills, and (3) develop and improve my ability to cope with change.

Other resources for assessment include Personal Skills Map (available through Life Skills Center, Corpus Christi, Texas) and Real Time 360 (available through Real Time Performance, www.realtimeperformance. com).

Use Worksheet 7 to list a career mission statement, a goal, and development objectives. Here's an example of how this worksheet may look when it's filled out:

WORKSHEET 7 Defining Development Objectives

Mission:

Goal:

Development objectives:

- *Mission:* Continually develop leadership and business management skills in order to lead my team more effectively and meet or exceed business goals
- *Goal:* Achieve a promotion to manage a business unit within the next year
- *Development objectives:* Improve my ability to think strategically, and develop skills to effectively lead change

This process of defining your mission, your goal, and your development objectives is the first step in preparing to enter into a mentoring or networking relationship. Don't worry if you're not sure what skills are required for a particular job. Keep in mind that your mentor can also help you clarify your goals and development needs.

IDENTIFY WAYS OTHERS CAN HELP

In this section, we'll look at how others can help you after you've identified your goals and needs. For example, let's say you want to get into management, and you've determined that you need to improve your leadership and influencing skills in order to achieve your goal. Obviously, you're going to look for help from someone who has strong leadership and influencing skills.

Consider all the ways a mentor can help. A mentor can provide coaching on a project or share how she leads and influences. You may even be able to observe your mentor in action. She can also suggest other resources, such as books, courses, and experts to talk to.

Now consider network contacts and all the ways they can help. If you want to work in management, for example, you're probably going to look for people who can have a positive influence on your chances of being selected as a manager. A network contact can give you introductions to influential people in the organization that you're targeting. He can put you in touch with hiring managers. He can put in a good word for you and maybe even suggest to a hiring manager that she consider you for a specific position.

Write down all the ways a mentor or network contact can help you achieve your specific goals and objectives. Come up with ideas for each objective (see Worksheet 8).

WORKSHEET 8 Getting Help to Meet Objectives

Objectives	**How a Mentor or Contact Can Help**
Objective 1	
Objective 2	
Objective 3	

If you determine how others can help you, you'll be prepared to take the next steps: finding and approaching mentors. (You'll learn more about this step in Chapter Five.)

PLAN YOUR NETWORKING STRATEGY

Your business or career mission statement is your foundation for getting started with mentoring and networking. Another approach is to attend networking events.

In addition to the groundwork of identifying goals and needs, there is preparation that you should do before attending a networking event, in order to get the most out of it:

- Learn about the event.
- Determine what you want to accomplish.
- Identify people you want to talk to or meet.
- Prepare and rehearse an introduction.
- Identify what you have to offer.

LEARN ABOUT THE EVENT

Learn everything you can about the event itself. Refer to the invitation. What type of event is it? Is it a sit-down meal or buffet? Will there be a speaker? Is it a trade show? How many people will be there? Will you introduce yourself to the whole audience, or will there be one-to-one introductions? How long is the event?

If this is your first time attending an event sponsored by an organization, learn more about the organization. Talk to a current member. What is the organization's mission? What is the profile of its members? What can you expect from this event? This information will help you plan your strategy.

DETERMINE WHAT YOU WANT TO ACCOMPLISH

Attend the event with a purpose in mind. What do you want to accomplish? Review your business or career goal and your development objectives. Keeping your goals in mind will help you gain the information and resources you need to accomplish them. What specific information do you need? If you're looking for a supplier, do you need recommendations? If you're looking for a job, do you need contacts? Do you want to qualify a prospective client?

What about your networking goals? This event may be a good opportunity to stay visible. Do you want to make new contacts in your field, or do you want to reconnect with people you already know? By understanding your goals for attending the event, you'll be more likely to fulfill them.

IDENTIFY PEOPLE YOU WANT TO TALK TO OR MEET

Think about the people who are likely to attend the event, and make a note of those you'd like to talk to. Is there someone with whom you would you like to reconnect and build a relationship? Is there someone you'd like to meet? Review your list of how others can provide assistance. What types of people would be in a position to help you achieve your goals? Again, if you think these questions through in advance, you're more likely to meet and talk to the right people.

PREPARE AND REHEARSE AN INTRODUCTION

Think about how you want to present yourself. When you introduce yourself to others, you have only about seven seconds to grab their attention and about thirty to make a lasting impression. The biggest mistake you can make is to introduce yourself by giving only your name, your title, and your company's name. If you just give people data, they can't relate to or connect with *you.* This is a missed opportunity! Instead, use a phrase or a tag line that captures people's attention, and share the value you bring to others.

Prepare your introduction by writing two or three sentences that tell others who you are and the value and benefit of what you do. Use simple, plain language that everyone can understand, and keep it succinct: it should take you no more than thirty seconds to introduce yourself. Your introduction should include the following elements:

- Your name
- Your company's name, if you choose to give it
- What you do
- The value you bring to others

Always use your first name and your last name. If your company is well known, mention it, but otherwise you may want to skip it and focus on what you do.

Always include the benefit of what you do. For example, instead of saying, "My name is Kathy, and I sell insurance," you might say, "I'm Kathy Smith, and I sell the peace of mind that comes with knowing you are protected from the unexpected." Isn't that more attention-getting? Here are some more sample introductions:

- "Good morning. I'm Bill Jones. I'm a chiropractor, and I help people lead lives free of pain and discomfort."
- "Hello. I'm Marlys Thompson. I work with people who want to create a life you love, in your business *and* in your personal life."
- "My name is Marc LeBlanc. I work with people who want to start a business and small-business owners who want to grow their business or professional practice."

When you prepare your introduction, start by reviewing your business or career mission statement. Then, to create a powerful and dynamic introduction, answer the questions in Worksheet 9, on the next page.

Practice your introduction until it flows smoothly and easily. Practice in front of the mirror, and then practice for family members and friends and get feedback. Rehearse your introduction until it comes naturally; you don't want it to come across canned.

IDENTIFY WHAT YOU HAVE TO OFFER

Networking is a two-way street: you receive help from others, and you offer others help. Many people underestimate the value they bring to others, but it's important to know yourself and what you have to offer and to realize that you can be a valuable resource. If you identify at the outset what you have to offer, you will be better prepared to build mutually supportive relationships with people you meet at networking events.

What do you have to offer? Do you have information, ideas, contacts, or other resources? I, for example, am a member of the National Speakers Association, a network of professional speakers, and many experienced speakers have helped me in my career.

WORKSHEET 9 Preparing an Introduction

What do I do?

What do I love most about what I do?

What value do I offer?

What problem does my product or service solve?

What difference does my product, service, or skill make in the lives of others?

What do I want to be known for?

My introduction:

In return, I can offer contacts at Hewlett-Packard Company, where I have worked for eighteen years and where many speakers and trainers are eager to give presentations.

Think about the ways in which you can offer assistance. Here are some ideas:

- Introduce your contacts to other people you know
- Refer business to people
- Send people information that may be of interest to them
- Encourage people
- Share your expertise
- Recommend products and services that have been of benefit to you
- Offer ideas and suggestions

SUMMARY

- You need to identify your business and career goals and your developmental needs before you can identify the best people to help you.
- Your business or career mission statement defines your purpose. It tells what you offer, to whom, and why it is of value.
- Your business or career goal identifies the result you want to achieve within a specific time frame.
- Once you have determined your goal, you can identify the knowledge, skills, or abilities you will need in order to reach it. State what you have to learn as your development objectives.
- For each objective, consider all the ways a mentor or network contact can help you achieve it.
- In order to get the most out of a networking event, plan your networking strategy. Learn about the event, determine what you want to accomplish, identify the people you want to meet or talk to, prepare and rehearse an introduction, and identify what you have to offer.
- Your introduction should include your name, perhaps your company's name, and what you do. A crucial element is the value you bring to others.
- You can provide valuable assistance to others by offering information, ideas, contacts, and other resources.

LEARNING TOOLS

1. Complete the following development assessment for mentees.

WORKSHEET 10 Development Assessment for Mentees

Review the knowledge, skills, and abilities below and rate each based on your need and desire to develop in that particular area.

	Low Need				High Need
Professionalism/understand perceptions	1	2	3	4	5
Planning and organization skills	1	2	3	4	5
Project management skills	1	2	3	4	5
Stress management	1	2	3	4	5
Balance work and personal demands	1	2	3	4	5
Understand culture and policies	1	2	3	4	5
Written communication skills	1	2	3	4	5
Team-building skills	1	2	3	4	5
Leadership skills	1	2	3	4	5
Interpersonal communication skills	1	2	3	4	5
Presentation skills	1	2	3	4	5
Negotiation skills	1	2	3	4	5

	Low Need				High Need
Sales skills	1	2	3	4	5
Decision-making skills	1	2	3	4	5
Adapt to change/coping skills	1	2	3	4	5
Effectively juggle many projects/tasks at once	1	2	3	4	5
Problem-solving skills	1	2	3	4	5
Technical competence in ______________	1	2	3	4	5
Network with ________ (group, company, field)	1	2	3	4	5
Other areas for development:					
______________________	1	2	3	4	5
______________________	1	2	3	4	5
______________________	1	2	3	4	5

2. Pick one to three development areas to focus on. Write them as objectives (see Worksheet 7, page 39).
3. For each objective, identify the ways in which a mentor or contact can help (see Worksheet 8, page 40).
4. Prepare your introduction (see Worksheet 9, page 44). Practice it out loud until it flows smoothly.

5. Use Worksheet 11 to prepare for an upcoming networking event.

WORKSHEET 11 Preparing for a Networking Event

What do I need to know about the event? What type of event is it? What will the format be? Who will attend?

What do I hope to accomplish by attending this event?

Who are the people I want to meet or reconnect with?

How will I introduce myself?

What do I have to offer?

CHAPTER 4

FINDING MENTORS & NETWORKING CONTACTS

Now that you've planned your strategy, you're ready to start looking for mentors and networking contacts. Once you've determined what you need, you can identify who can meet those needs and where to find these helpers. Let's look first at potential mentors. What should you look for in a mentor?

WHAT TO LOOK FOR IN A POTENTIAL MENTOR

First and foremost, your mentor should have the knowledge, skills, and expertise that you need. There has to be a good match between your development needs and the background, skills, and experience of the mentor. Ask yourself, or ask others, "Who has the expertise I need to learn from?"

Besides the more obvious requirement of having particular expertise, there are a number of other qualities to look for in a mentor. Here are some questions to ask yourself as you think of potential mentors:

- Who is successful in my field?
- Whom do I admire and respect?
- Who are the most influential people I know?
- Who thinks I have potential?
- Who has encouraged me?
- Who has helped me in the past and might help again?

Start by making a list of potential mentors. List people who are successful or influential in your field and whom you admire and respect. For each one, identify what it is you admire about him or her and what he or she has achieved that you would like to achieve for yourself. Then, using Worksheet 12, consider other characteristics of your potential mentors.

WORKSHEET 12 Assessing a Potential Mentor's Characteristics

My potential mentor . . .	Yes	Not Sure	No
Has achieved a level of responsibility or recognition that I want to achieve			
Possesses the knowledge, skills, expertise I need			
Is influential in my organization or field			
Is someone I respect, admire, and trust			
Is willing to invest the time to mentor people			
Listens to understand others' points of view			
Encourages people to achieve their goals			
Has excellent coaching skills			

Good mentors possess certain qualities, but keep in mind that it is difficult to find a single mentor who has them all. Therefore, you'll need to determine which ones are most important to you.

If "Yes" was your response for all the characteristics in Worksheet 12, then you are fortunate; you have identified a good mentor. If your response was "Not Sure" for a few of the characteristics, don't rule out this potential mentor; understand which characteristics are most important to you. You can still have an effective relationship as long as your response was "Yes" for the most important characteristics.

ACHIEVEMENT

Look for a mentor who has achieved a level of responsibility or recognition that represents what you want to achieve. Who has been successful in your field? Who has achieved what you want to achieve? For example, Heather Shea, whom we met in Chapter One, sought out Tom Peters. She had read *In Search of Excellence* and knew that she wanted to work for this book's coauthor. As a very successful business consultant, author, and speaker, Peters was a role model for Heather, even before he knew that she existed. Heather wanted to emulate his success.

We learn best from example. Your mentor can act as a role model and set a positive example for you. You can learn not just from your mentor's successes but also from his or her failures.

KNOWLEDGE, SKILLS, AND EXPERTISE

Your mentor should have the knowledge, skills, and expertise that you identified in your needs assessment. Look for a good match between your developmental needs and your potential mentor's expertise. A knowledgeable, skilled mentor can provide one-to-one instruction by sharing information and discussing processes (for example, by telling how he goes about managing a project or marketing his products).

INFLUENCE

Look for a mentor who is influential in her organization or field. Does she have access to people and situations that can benefit your career development? A mentor who is in the professional "loop" can offer many more opportunities. Through her connections, she can introduce you to other important people, and they in turn can help you advance in your career or build your business.

An influential mentor can act as a sponsor or advocate who provides opportunities to promote your career. Is your potential mentor in a position to give you visibility? He can open doors for you by inviting you to attend important meetings, allowing you to give an important presentation, giving you challenging assignments, or asking you to coauthor an article or book.

KATHLEEN BARTON A few years ago, my mentor, Linda Phillips-Jones, was unable to speak at a women's conference because of a schedule conflict. She asked me if I would speak in her place. I was flattered that she had confidence that I could fill her shoes. She then recommended me to the program director and assured her that she would not be disappointed. This speaking opportunity gave me exposure and helped jump-start my business. I received new business as a result of speaking at this conference and was even invited back to speak the next year.

ABILITY TO INSPIRE RESPECT, ADMIRATION, AND TRUST

Look for someone who has your respect, admiration, and trust. These are important elements of a successful mentoring relationship. Who has your respect? Who has qualities and characteristics that you admire? Who is someone you'd like to emulate?

Trust is the foundation of a successful mentoring relationship. Is your potential mentor honest and trustworthy? Do you feel comfortable with her? It's important that you have similar values because shared values encourage a more trusting and honest relationship. Are you comfortable discussing your priorities with her? If you are uneasy about a potential mentor's values, then it's not a good match, no matter how influential or successful she is. Someone who has climbed the ladder of success but left "dead bodies" along the way is not likely to be a good mentor for you.

WILLINGNESS TO INVEST TIME

A good mentor is willing to invest time. Most professionals are extremely busy, but the best mentors know the value of mentoring, and they make it a priority.

Even if your potential mentor seems very busy, don't let it discourage you. Mentoring may take less time than you think. Mentoring can be effective in as little as two hours a month.

Nevertheless, you do need to consider the circumstances of your potential mentor's life. Has he recently started a new job or business? Is he in transition or under a lot of pressure right now? If so, the time may not be right for him to enter into a mentoring relationship.

LISTENING SKILLS

How well does your potential mentor listen? Good mentors are good listeners. They take the time to listen, and they give you their full attention. They ask questions. They listen in order to fully understand your point of view. They paraphrase to confirm that they have understood. Such attention makes you feel important. Does your potential mentor listen more than he talks? Good mentors are more interested in you than in talking about themselves.

ABILITY TO BE ENCOURAGING

A good mentor is encouraging. We all need a cheerleader, someone to encourage and support us. The best mentors believe in their mentees' potential. "He believed in me even when I did not believe in myself," says Heather Shea of Tom Peters.

Who has encouraged you? Encouragement helps build your confidence to pursue and achieve your goals. Who believes you have potential? Who would believe you had potential if he or she knew you?

Good mentors express positive expectations about their mentees and give positive reinforcement. Carlene Ellis of Intel says her first mentor was her dad, a strawberry farmer in the South. "He raised me to believe that I could be CEO of IBM," she says. "He gave me the strength to believe that I could be anything I wanted."

COACHING SKILLS

Look for a mentor who has excellent coaching skills. As a coach, she can assist you with your strategy. She can help you prepare for a challenging situation by talking it through with you or even by role-playing the anticipated scenario. A good coach can also help you debrief a challenging situation by getting your perspective, giving positive and constructive feedback, and offering suggestions for how to improve next time. A good coach gives feedback that is timely, direct, specific, neutral, and, above all, helpful. What about your potential mentor? Does she have good coaching skills?

KATHLEEN BARTON Several years ago, I worked as a diversity program manager. In my role, it was important that I be able to influence change. Because I was new in my role, I wanted to develop the skills of a change agent. I wanted to be able to read the environment and work within it to get things done. I also wanted to be able to influence people and be politically savvy. I sought a mentor who could help me develop these skills. I asked my colleagues who they thought was a really strong change agent.

A number of responses pointed to the same person: Ken Larson, a very influential human resources manager in our organization. I had worked with Ken previously on a project, and he was someone I trusted and respected. He was also a very good coach. I initiated a mentoring relationship, and Ken was indeed insightful. I learned a lot from him in this fruitful mentoring partnership.

WHERE TO LOOK FOR POTENTIAL MENTORS

After brainstorming potential mentors and assessing the characteristics of each one, refine your list to arrive at a final group of potential mentors. You should have several names on this final list: for mentoring to be most effective, you'll need to draw on the expertise of multiple mentors.

What if you don't know anyone who would make a good mentor for you? What if you don't know anyone who has the particular expertise that you are looking for? (For example, maybe you want to become skilled at creating Web pages, but you don't know anyone with that expertise.) What if you don't know anyone who has achieved what you want to achieve? (Maybe you want to start your own grocery delivery service, but you don't know of anyone who has done something similar.) This is the time to do some networking and research.

NETWORKING

Start your search for a mentor by asking around. Use your network to get recommendations for potential mentors. You may be thinking that this is all new to you, and that you don't have a network. But you already do, whether you believe it or not. Think about all the people you grew up with, went to school with, worked with, met through friends or at church, and so forth. Donna Fisher, in *People Power,* reports that people have anywhere from 250 to 3,000 contacts.

Here are people you can consult:

- Co-workers
- Members of professional associations and organizations
- Professors
- Family members
- Friends
- Fellow church members

You might start with your co-workers, especially if you want a mentor from your current organization. It's often very helpful to have a mentor from your own organization, especially if you are a new employee or see a long-term future with the organization. An internal mentor can clue you in to the internal politics of the organization and teach you the unwritten rules. Nevertheless, it may also be very helpful to find a mentor outside your organization. Sometimes we get ingrained in our own company's way of thinking or doing things, and it may be helpful to get an outside perspective.

Don't stop with your co-workers. Ask everyone you know if they can tell you about others who might be good mentors for you. Join professional organizations and associations in your field, and attend meetings to meet people. You will probably get to know people who can be suitable mentors.

RESEARCH

In addition to networking, you can also do research, using these and other resources:

- Your local library
- The Internet
- Career placement services and counselors
- Colleges and associations
- Trade journals and other publications

Check your local library or the Internet to do some research. Find out who the experts are in your field or in the skill areas that you have identified. *Who's Who* publications list the names of people who are considered leaders in their fields; geographically based versions of these volumes are also available.

Check with a career placement service or career counselors. These career professionals often refer their clients to people in particular fields that the clients are seeking to enter. Your local college can be another resource. Check with professors, deans, and the career center for referrals.

Finally, check trade journals and books in your field. Read articles, study the bibliographies of books, and read about authors. People who are published are generally considered to be experts, and they carry influence.

Your search may lead you to potential mentors who live in other parts of the country, but don't let geography limit you, especially if you want to develop an uncommon kind of expertise or business (such as a circus performing-arts school).

A local mentor is ideal because he or she is more accessible. You can meet in person, and it's generally easier to build a relationship that way. But remote mentoring can also be effective. The telephone, e-mail, fax machines, and the Internet make remote mentors more accessible. If your job requires you to travel, you may even be able to meet your mentor in person.

FORMAL PROGRAMS

You might also consider some formal programs established to match mentors and mentees. There are several available for particular groups and professions, and some are available on the Internet for "e-mentoring." Here are just a few of the programs.

FOR PROFESSIONALS

- Perfect Personnel, which searches for professional mentors all over the globe to assist individuals in their careers (www.beverlynb.bizland.com)

FOR WOMEN

- Menttium 100, a project designed to help fast-track women hook up with mentors outside their own companies (www.menttium.com)
- The Woman to Woman Mentoring Program, which matches women who have experience in business, computer applications, and other areas to provide the best learning experiences (www.womensresourcentr.org/mentor)
- Electra's Mentoring Connection, where women who are beginning or changing their careers can find experienced professional women to guide them (www.mentor.electra.com/electra)

FOR PEOPLE OF COLOR

- Menttium, a cross-company program for fast-track professionals of color (www.menttium.com)

FOR SMALL-BUSINESS OWNERS

- The Small Business Administration, a program for people starting a new business who want an experienced business owner to guide them

NETWORKING CONTACTS: WHOM DO YOU WANT TO MEET?

Now that you know what to look for in a mentor and where to find mentors, let's turn our attention to networking contacts. As with mentors, it's helpful to target the types of people who can be most helpful to you. Begin by making a list of people you want to meet. Refer again to your business or career mission statement (see Chapter Three). List potential clients or customers, potential employers, and people in your field. Brainstorm as many as you can. Anyone you want to do business with or work for is a candidate for your list. If you want to change jobs, make a list of people who could be instrumental in helping you make that happen. List people in and outside your company, service providers, customers, and others in your industry.

HOW TO MEET CONTACTS

Start with your own network, which you've already established. Do you know anyone who knows someone you want to meet? If a mutual friend or contact can introduce you, that is ideal. If you can't think of anyone, don't worry; keep in mind the rule of "six degrees of separation." This rule is based on the theory that if you take the people you know, and if they consider the people they know, and so on, you and everyone else on earth are at most just six people away from knowing every other person (see Pool and Kochen, "Contacts and Influence").

BB Hill, principal consultant of Organization Development Associates, had always wanted to meet Jack Canfield, author of *Chicken Soup for the Soul.* BB attended a writers' conference on Maui, in Hawaii, where she met John Ball for coffee and told him she wanted to meet Canfield.

John said, "I met Jack in the hot tub last night," and he added that Canfield was looking for stories for upcoming books. "Go hunt him down," he suggested.

BB found Canfield at the conference, introduced herself, and gave him two stories, which she hopes will be published soon in one of his new books.

Whom do you want to meet? Someone in information technology at Intel? An NBC news anchor? A well-known author? Try asking people you know. You may be surprised at the results!

WHERE TO MEET CONTACTS

Think about the interests and needs of the people you want to meet. What organizations or clubs are targeted to their interests and goals? For example, if you want to meet technical types, consider one of the many organizations for people in engineering and information technology. There are even organizations for subgroups of this population, such as the Society of Women Engineers and the National Society of Black Engineers.

List possible organizations where you can meet potential clients or employers. Also consider organizations in which you can meet people who will be able to introduce you to potential clients or employers. Here are some possibilities:

- Industry associations
- Professional organizations
- Networking groups
- College and fraternity alumni groups
- Education groups

- Chambers of commerce
- Civic organizations
- Philanthropic organizations
- Social clubs
- Research organizations in your particular industry or profession (check with your local library or on the Internet; a good resource is the *National Trade & Professional Organizations* directory)

JOINING ORGANIZATIONS In order to build your network, it is essential to join organizations and get involved. Join organizations where you are likely to meet the kinds of people you want to have in your network. Many people join organizations without giving much thought to how beneficial membership will be to them. Since no one has unlimited time, however, it helps to think this step through and be strategic about the organizations you join. Some people fret about the money they spend on organization memberships that offer no measurable return. Wasting money in this way can be especially painful for those who are self-employed or unemployed, since membership dues are an out-of-pocket cost for them.

If you're thinking of joining an organization, go to one of its meetings, and then use the following questions to decide whether you should join:

- Is the mission of the organization aligned with your needs?
- If the organization features presenters, can you learn from them?
- Does the organization attract the type of people you want to meet?
- Are its functions well attended?
- Did you feel comfortable at the meeting?
- Do you like the mix of people?

- Were the members interested in getting to know you?
- Is the meeting time convenient?
- Are the membership dues and other costs affordable?

GETTING INVOLVED Once you've decided to join an organization, get involved! Attend all the functions: lunches, awards ceremonies, annual dinners, fund-raisers, and so on. Become visible, and meet a lot of people. Go to the national conventions and trade shows, and you'll be able to expand your network nationally. This can be a great advantage if you travel a lot.

More important, get involved in a small group. Join a committee, lead a special project, or volunteer for a position on the organization's board of directors. You're only going to get so much out of attending the monthly luncheons; you'll get more from participating in team activities, and that's also the best way to get to know people professionally, since your teammates will gain firsthand experience of you. They will become aware of your skills and know what results you've achieved, and they will learn that they can count on you. As a result, they'll be more likely to refer you to prospective clients or employers.

SUMMARY

- There has to be a good match between your development needs and the background, skills, and experience of your potential mentor.
- Make a list of potential mentors by considering people who are successful or influential in your field, and whom you admire and respect.
- Good mentors have a number of characteristics. These include achievement, skills, expertise, influence, trustworthiness, a willingness to invest time, good listening skills, the ability to offer encouragement, and good coaching skills.
- Conduct your search for a mentor by asking for recommendations from people you know, conducting research to find experts in your field, or considering a formal mentoring program that suits your needs.
- To build your network, start by identifying people you want to meet. Make a list of potential clients or customers, potential employers, and experts in your field.
- The "six degrees of separation" rule states that you are only six people away from anybody you want to meet, anywhere in the world.
- Identify organizations where you may be able to meet potential clients or employers.
- Build your network by joining organizations and getting involved.

LEARNING TOOLS

1. Using Worksheet 13, make a list of potential mentors. List people who are successful or influential in your field and whom you admire and respect. For each person, list what you admire about him or her and what he or she has achieved that you yourself would like to achieve.

WORKSHEET 13 Assessing Potential Mentors

Successful or Influential Person	What I Admire	His or Her Achievements I Want to Emulate

2. Using Worksheet 12 (page 50), assess your potential mentors. If you've indicated "Yes" for all the characteristics, then you have identified a mentor with whom you can have an effective mentoring partnership. If you've indicated "Not sure" for just a few of the characteristics, don't rule out this potential mentor; just understand which characteristics are most important to you. You may still be able to have an effective relationship as long as you've indicated "Yes" for the most important characteristics.
3. Test the "six degrees of separation" rule! Identify a person you want to meet or do business with, a company to which you want access, or a type of business to which you want access. Be proactive: share this information with six people, and see what results you get.

4. To build your network, use Worksheet 14 to create a plan for initiating relationships. In the first column, list potential clients or customers, potential employers, and so on. In the second column, list people you know who are already in contact with the people in column one. In the third column, list the settings where you can meet your desired contacts, including organizations that are targeted to their interests and needs.

WORKSHEET 14 Plan for Initiating Relationships

Person I want to meet	People I already know who are in contact with this person	Settings where I can find this person
1.		
2.		
3.		

CHAPTER 5

APPROACHING MENTORS & CONTACTS

Now that you know where to find mentors and networking contacts, you're ready to initiate contact with those who are in a position to help you. This can cause great anxiety for some people: they don't feel comfortable initiating relationships, they may not know how to approach people to ask for help, or they fear being rejected.

But the fastest way to grow professionally is to take risks and learn as you go. Eleanor Roosevelt said that the only way to conquer fear is to do what you fear and keep doing it until you develop a series of successful experiences. So take a small step by approaching someone to initiate a helping relationship. The rest of this chapter will show you how.

OVERCOMING RESISTANCE

There are two common barriers that people typically face when they want to initiate helping relationships: reluctance to ask for help and not knowing how to approach someone for help.

RELUCTANCE TO ASK FOR HELP

Many people are reluctant to ask for help. They don't want to impose on someone else. They may feel that other people are too busy to make time for them. They may fear that others will perceive them as weak or needy if they ask for help. Most common of all is the fear of being rejected: if another person turns us down, we may take it personally and conclude that he or she does not really like us or does not think we're good enough. Carolyn Duff, author of *Learning from Other Women,* discusses fear of rejection in her book. A woman in one of her focus groups said, "I would feel so deflated and defeated if I approached a woman to learn from her and she refused me!" This concern was expressed by women of all ages.

If you share some of these fears, remind yourself why you are looking for people to help you. What is the most compelling reason that you identified for building your mentor network? Let that reason motivate you to step out of your comfort zone.

NOT KNOWING HOW TO APPROACH SOMEONE FOR HELP

Many people don't know how to ask for help. Not only are they fearful of initiating relationships; they also lack confidence in their ability to do so. They are not sure what to do, and they don't want to look foolish.

HOW TO APPROACH MENTORS

Before we discuss how to approach a mentor, let's consider the steps that should *not* be taken.

WHAT NOT TO DO

This may come as a surprise to you, but don't come right out and ask someone, "Will you be my mentor?" The word *mentor* can be a loaded one. Some of the people you approach may feel apprehensive; maybe they don't think of themselves as mentors, or they fear that mentoring will require a large commitment on their part and are not sure if they can make such a commitment. Others may not be sure of what you are asking; people have different definitions of the term *mentor*. Therefore, avoid using the term unless you define what you mean. Instead, make a specific request (we'll discuss this point a little later).

Don't act desperate. Don't come on too strong, or you may scare off a potential mentor. But don't be too apologetic, either. Some people tend to use disclaimers: "If it isn't too much trouble . . . ," "If you have the time. . . ." Statements like these make you sound weak, and the other person may think he or she would be wasting time with you. Instead, be more assertive in how you ask for help.

Don't get discouraged. If someone says no, ask another potential mentor. Harvey MacKay, author of *Dig Your Well Before You're Thirsty,* says, "One reason that people are afraid to network is that they don't want to hear the word 'no.' But 'no' is the second best answer there is. At least you know where you stand." Persistence pays off: one person may turn you down, but there are others who will be willing to help.

WHAT TO DO: A SIX-STEP APPROACH

Here is a tested approach to getting someone's agreement to be your mentor:

1. Research the potential mentor's background.
2. Make contact.
3. Make a specific request.
4. Meet with your potential mentor.
5. Follow up.
6. Ask to meet on a continuing basis.

STEP 1: RESEARCH THE POTENTIAL MENTOR'S BACKGROUND First do your homework. Approach this task as you would an important job interview. Find out everything you can about your potential mentor: her work, interests, and needs. Find out what, if anything, has been written by or about this person. Review any articles or books she has written. Review work she has designed or produced. Talk to others who know her. The more background you have on your potential mentor, the easier it will be to approach her and establish a relationship.

STEP 2: MAKE CONTACT After doing your homework, you'll want to enlist the help of a mutual friend or acquaintance. This help can take any of several forms:

- *Your friend or colleague can introduce you in person.* This is the best option. It gives you a chance to meet and get to know the other person face to face.
- *Your friend or colleague can put in a good word for you.* He or she mentions your name and says something positive about you to the prospective mentor.
- *Your friend or colleague can call the potential mentor.* He or she mentions you to your prospective mentor and says you'd like to make contact.

It is always best to have an introduction rather than go in cold; you're more likely to be well received.

If you can, have a face-to-face meeting with your potential mentor before asking for help. It's easier to make a connection that way. One of the most effective strategies is to get involved in business situations with your potential mentor. For example, attend a meeting of a professional organization or association to which your potential mentor belongs. (If you've done your homework, you already know which organizations these are.) At the meeting, introduce yourself, and pursue small talk about an area of interest to your potential mentor. Volunteer to work on a task force or committee with him or her. This commitment allows you to demonstrate your skills in action.

STEP 3: MAKE A SPECIFIC REQUEST Now you're ready to request some advice and feedback from your potential mentor. Start by giving some positive feedback: compliment or congratulate her in some way. This is an opportunity for you to let her know what you admire about her and hope to learn from her. You might say, "You're really good at leading projects. It's really helped me to be a part of this team and see how you lead meetings. Would it be okay if I came to you for advice on my project?" Try to make your request as specific as possible, and keep it simple. You can ask for advice on your business or your career, or you can ask for feedback on your performance. Here are some more examples:

- "You have a successful and growing business. And I know you're well regarded by your clients. I'd like to get your advice on how to develop client relationships."
- "You have a strong marketing background, and I value your opinion. I'm trying to decide if I should go into market research or marketing communications. I'd like to get your reactions and feedback."
- "I've read your books, and I really like your writing style. Would you be willing to review an article I've written for publication?"

If you're considering a career change, you might ask for an informational interview. This allows you to learn directly about a specific job or career from someone doing the job. For example, you might ask a potential mentor who is a financial planner, "I'm interested in becoming a financial planner. Could we meet for about half an hour so I can find out more about what you do?"

Be sure to consider what you can offer in exchange. Remember, mentoring is a two-way street; if you can do something for your potential mentor, then mention it, by all means. You might offer to take your potential mentor out to lunch or breakfast in exchange for seeking his perspective on a particular topic. One creative mentee, June Davidson, offered to sell products at the back of the room for Paul Karasik, a speaker and the author of *How to Make It Big in the Seminar Business.* In return, he offered her tips and advice on getting started in offering seminars. Today June is president of the American Seminar Leaders Association.

When requesting time with your potential mentor, make it as convenient for him as possible. Be flexible about when and where you meet. Be sure to keep the initial meeting brief—say, half an hour or so, but never more than an hour. Be respectful of your potential mentor's time.

STEP 4: MEET WITH YOUR POTENTIAL MENTOR Once you've succeeded in getting your specific request accepted, you're ready to meet with your potential mentor. Never go in cold to this meeting! Set goals, and identify desired outcomes. Prepare a list of questions. Your potential mentor will be impressed with your preparation and organization.

During the meeting, stay focused on your potential mentor. In order to break the ice, it is useful to get him to talk about himself. If you're interested in learning about his career or business, you might say, "You've done much of what I hope to accomplish someday. How did you do it? How did you get started?" Listen attentively. Take notes. Ask your prepared questions, and seek specific suggestions. Be sure to consider any advice you're given.

STEP 5: FOLLOW UP After the meeting, try out some of your potential mentor's suggestions. You may find that they work out well, and you may ask yourself, "Why didn't I think of that?" Be prepared to share the results with him.

Follow up by sending a thank-you note or calling to say thanks. A handwritten note is more meaningful because of the time put into writing it, and because it can be saved. Let your potential mentor know how much you appreciate his taking the time to meet with you. Comment on something in particular he said that was significant to you, and let him know how valuable the advice was. In particular, tell him the results of any suggestions that you tried. This information will help him understand how beneficial the interaction was for you.

If it's appropriate, also send a small gift. You might enclose an article, a book, or an audiotape related to something you discussed, or you can be more creative. If he loves to play golf, you might include some golf balls or tees. Your gift shows him that you really listened and that you are thoughtful.

The purpose of following up is to demonstrate to your potential mentor how helpful he has been—that is, how you are already learning and gaining value. The interaction can also demonstrate how the relationship can be mutually beneficial. Once the mentor understands how you have benefited and how he can also benefit from your interactions, he is more likely to continue providing assistance. This opens the door for you to ask for further advice and feedback.

STEP 6: ASK TO MEET ON A CONTINUING BASIS At this point, your potential mentor has had a chance not only to meet and interact with you but also to see the value of what he can provide. Now you're ready to broach the subject of a mentoring relationship. Let your potential mentor know how helpful he has been, and tell him how much you think you could learn from him in the future. Mention the goals you have for your career, or the skills you want to develop. Suggest meeting with him on a regular basis—say, monthly or biweekly—or ask permission to get help on an ad hoc basis. Again, keep your request simple and specific. Here are some examples:

- "I've taken so much from our time together. Would you be open to meeting once a month for lunch? I would love to get your advice on the most important goals I've set and the decisions I'm facing."
- "You've been so helpful on this project. May I come to you for advice on my future projects?"
- "You've given me excellent feedback on my first chapter. Would you be willing to review each chapter of my book as I write it?"

Assure your potential mentor that you will be respectful of his time and job priorities. Answer any questions or concerns that he might have, but don't pressure him into an immediate decision.

There are many advantages to this approach. When this is followed, a potential mentor understands what you're asking and expecting, and she knows that you're serious about your development. She sees how helpful she has been to you, how much you appreciate her help, and how she can be of further help to you. She trusts that you will respect her time and that she, too, will benefit from the mentoring relationship. People are more willing to help when these conditions are present.

SANTIAGO RODRIGUEZ

The late Santiago Rodriguez of Microsoft told of his experience at a previous company. "When I started at Apple Computer," he said, "there were a few people I met right away who impressed me. I asked each of them, 'Would you mind being a mentor for me?' and I defined the term *mentor.* A mentor, I explained, was not someone who would tell me how to do my work. 'I want to use you as a sounding board,' I said. 'I want to run some ideas past you and find out if they make sense in this environment.' I said that my job was to be a change agent. I told them I needed allies and supporters: I was the content expert, I said, but I might not have the best ideas about how to implement my policies or programs.

"I suggested that, over the next two months, we touch base every two weeks for an hour. Then, if there was mutual interest, we could continue to meet.

"I met with my mentors for more than a year. They were invaluable and proved crucial to my success at Apple Computer."

Santiago added, "You don't have to wait for a formal mentoring program. When you ask, most people are flattered. But you need to be specific about what you mean. Have a job description for the mentor. Understand each of your roles."

By following the six-step process outlined here, you will be most likely to succeed in gaining a mentor's support. This process may seem a bit daunting at first, but you'll be more successful if you use it. Remember, you're asking someone to invest his or her most valuable resource—time—in your future. You need to convince your potential mentor that an investment of precious time will be worth the effort.

Some potential mentors may have to reject your request, and this response may have nothing to do with you. It may have to do with their circumstances. People may decline because of work pressure or commitments to mentor others, or because they don't think they have the expertise you need. If your request is rejected, don't get discouraged. Ask a potential mentor if he or she can recommend anyone else. Try again with another potential mentor. You're bound to succeed eventually.

HOW TO APPROACH CONTACTS: MEETING NEW PEOPLE

Now let's turn our attention to networking. How do you meet new people and make new contacts? How do you approach people at networking events and initiate conversation? What do you say after you introduce yourself?

For some people, particularly introverts, taking the initiative to meet new people can be nerve-racking. But these tips and ideas can make it easier for you.

DO YOUR HOMEWORK

When you know you're going to meet someone new, find out everything you can about him or her. Call that person's office and request a bio. If he or she is well known, read up on him or her. Talk to people who know the person. Look for anything that you have in common. The point is to help you build a relationship based on shared interests.

"I always make a special effort to inquire about people I'm going to meet and want to get to know better," says Harvey MacKay. In *Dig Your Well Before You're Thirsty,* Harvey gives this example:

> Recently, in Chicago, I appeared on a television round-table discussion sponsored by *Chief Executive* magazine. There were ten participants, [all] CEOs of companies. I knew the magazine had bios on all ten participants, because they had me send in mine, so I called and asked them to fax me materials on the rest of the panel, which they graciously did.
>
> Now I was prepared to prepare. One of the CEOs was born in my mother's hometown of Virginia, Minnesota. Bingo. When we were introduced, the first thing I did was ask him whether he'd ever had a chocolate soda as good as the ones that Ben Milavitz's Drug Store, a Virginia legend, used to make. Total amazement and instant credibility.

INITIATE CONVERSATION

When attending a meeting or event, you can take a passive role and hope that others will approach you, or you can take a proactive role and approach other people. Take the initiative: approach people, introduce yourself, and start a conversation. But how?

PRETEND TO BE THE HOST If you were the host and these strangers were guests in your home, what would you do? You would welcome them, of course. Do the same at this business event. Arrive early and meet the organizers. You'll feel more comfortable than if you were entering a room full of strangers. You will also have a chance to feel comfortable in the environment before the event begins.

When people start to arrive, approach and greet them. Make them feel welcome. Throughout the event, search out people who are alone. Give them special attention. Introduce yourself, and help them feel welcome. With this approach, you're making a mind shift and turning the tables. Act as if you were comfortable and confident, and you will come across that way. You'll find that people respond with a smile, an introduction, and a handshake.

ASK TO PLAY A ROLE IN THE EVENT Some people feel more comfortable if they have a job to do, such as handling registration, passing out materials, or serving refreshments. Roles like these allow you to mingle easily with people and give you something to do so you won't feel as awkward.

INTRODUCE YOURSELF Remember the introduction you prepared back in Chapter Three? Here is your opportunity to use it. If you have prepared a good introduction, you are able to share who you are and what you have to offer in a way that captures people's attention. You also should have practiced your introduction until it flows smoothly. The key is to come across naturally. A good introduction will help you connect with people, spark interest, and open the door to further conversation.

Janet Drez has found a creative way to capture people's attention. When she introduces herself, she says, "It is my passion to help women start and successfully grow any imaginable home-based business. For myself as well as the people I work with, there's no place like home." As she speaks, people can't help noticing her ruby slippers and ruby earrings. "They're conversation starters," Janet says. "People always ask me about the shoes." The slippers and earrings help her connect with others. "They get a taste of who I am—upbeat, enthusiastic, and fun."

You should not only introduce yourself but also introduce people you know to others. In addition to giving their names, say a thing or two about them: what they do, how you know them, and so forth. This kind of comment offers a starting point for conversation. You act as a catalyst to help other people meet new contacts.

HOW TO ESTABLISH RAPPORT: GETTING TO KNOW PEOPLE

Once you introduce yourself, you'll want to connect with others by getting to know them. You can establish rapport by showing interest in other people, calling them by name, asking questions, and listening.

BE INTERESTED IN OTHER PEOPLE

After you introduce yourself, what do you say? Rather than worry about what you're going to say, focus on what others are saying. If you focus your attention on someone other than yourself, you will reduce your self-consciousness. When you give people your attention, they are more likely to remember and appreciate you. Dale Carnegie summed it up best in *How to Win Friends and Influence People:* "You can make more friends in two months by becoming really interested in other people than you can in two years by trying to get other people interested in you. Which is just another way of saying that the way to make a friend is to be one."

Be genuinely interested in other people, and show concern for them. I think here of my pastor, David George. He is very warm, personable, and authentic. When he asks, "How are you?" he really wants to know. He's not just extending a greeting; he is genuinely interested. People feel good after talking with him. His whole manner shows that he cares.

CALL PEOPLE BY NAME

One way to show interest in other people is to use and remember their names. People appreciate it when you remember their names, especially at a later date. Pay attention as people introduce themselves so that you can use their names and remember them for the future.

Have you ever just been introduced to someone and immediately forgotten the person's name? It can be embarrassing. I must admit that I am not very good with names, and so I make a conscious effort to remember them. Here are some tips that have helped me:

- When you meet someone, take a look at his or her name tag (if he or she is wearing one). Seeing the name in print (a visual cue) as well as hearing it (an auditory cue) will help you remember it because the information is coming in through more than one of your five senses.
- Associate the person's name with something else. For example, if I'm meeting someone with the same name as someone else I already know, then I associate the new person with the one I know. Or I might associate the person's name with one of his or her prominent features (Laura, pretty blue eyes; Jim, big man; Julie, red hair; Brian, mustache).
- Repeat the person's name throughout your conversation. The more times you say the name, the more likely you are to remember it.
- Repeat the person's name when ending the conversation.

ASK QUESTIONS AND LISTEN

We've probably all been cornered by someone who loves to talk about himself, and all we're thinking about is how to escape. If you find yourself saying "I" a lot, it's time to listen for a while. In fact, we should listen more than we talk. As I always like to say, God gave us one mouth and two ears!

One of the best ways to show interest in other people is to ask questions and listen to the answers. Ask open-ended questions that encourage others to talk about themselves, their work, and their accomplishments. Most people love talking about themselves. Here are some questions to ask:

- What do you do?
- What do you love most about your work?
- What do you most enjoy about being a member of this organization?
- What do you like to do when you're not working?

Ask follow-up questions that are tailored to the person's previous responses. When you truly listen, you communicate to others that they are important. Here are some guidelines for listening from Donna Fisher, author of *People Power:*

- Show interest in people and what they are saying.
- Make eye contact and focus on the other person.
- Give your full attention to what is being said.
- Be eager to learn something from the conversation.
- Listen with the intent of gathering information, connecting, and developing rapport.
- Listen for commonalities.

Most of the time, we are so focused on what we are going to say next that we don't really listen to the other person, or we allow our mind to wander (that is easy to do because we can think much faster than we can speak). But we need to turn off the conversations we have in our head and truly focus on other people. Listening gives us clues about what to say or ask next.

Listen with a purpose. That will help you avoid the wandering mind trap. Listen to learn more about others: who they are, what they do, and how you can help them. Listen for opportunities to be a resource and to offer ideas or contacts. Also listen for things you and others have in common. That will help you make connections. People feel more comfortable with people with whom they have something in common

The evangelist Billy Graham is a master networker. When he meets someone for the first time, he makes him or her feel like the most important person in the room. He makes and maintains eye contact. He smiles. He listens. When he talks, he asks questions or makes comments that show he is hearing and is interested in what the person has to say. He also gives the person a chance to make a point without being interrupted.

SUMMARY

- There are two common barriers to initiating a helping relationship: reluctance to ask for help, and not knowing how to approach someone for help.
- In approaching mentors, avoid using the term *mentor* without defining it. Don't act desperate or apologetic, and don't get discouraged.
- Follow the six-step approach outlined in this chapter to gain a mentor's support: research his or her background, make contact, make a specific request, meet, follow up, and ask for regular meetings.
- The advantages of using the six-step approach are that mentors understand what you're asking for, how they can help, how much you appreciate them and their time, and how they themselves can benefit.
- When you know you're going to meet someone new, find out everything you can about him or her.
- Take the initiative to approach people, introduce yourself, and start conversations.
- Make connections and establish rapport by showing interest in other people, calling them by name, asking questions, and listening.

LEARNING TOOLS

1. Research the background of one potential mentor or networking contact. Treat this exercise as an investigation. Find out everything you can about this person: his or her work, interests, and needs. Request a bio from his or her business. Find out what, if anything, has been written by or about this person, and review it. Study work that he or she has designed or produced. Talk to others who know this person.

2. Pick one potential mentor or networking contact. Identify how you plan to make contact with this person: through an introduction by way of a mutual friend, colleague, or acquaintance? by joining a professional organization or attending a meeting that your potential mentor or contact is likely to attend? by volunteering to help on a project or committee to which this person has made a commitment? in some other way?

3. Plan how you will ask for help from your potential mentor. Tell your potential mentor what you admire about him and what you hope to learn from him. Make a specific request for advice, feedback, and the like. ("I hear that you're one of the best sales representatives in the company. I'm interested in getting into sales. Would you be willing to meet for breakfast or lunch so I can find out more about what you do?") Write your request here:

____

____

____

____

____

4. At the next meeting or event you attend, pretend you are the host. Approach people, greet them, and introduce yourself. Stretch yourself. See if you can do this with five to seven new people.

5. Practice calling people by name and remembering their names. Try to use a new person's name at least three times in your conversation. Come up with an association (such as a prominent feature) to help you remember the person's name. After attending a meeting or event, see if you can remember five new contacts' names.

CHAPTER 6

BUILDING RELATIONSHIPS

Let's say you've secured a mentor's help or made a connection with a new contact. Now what? How do you get started?

Start by building the relationship. This is crucial: people who are more task oriented tend to overlook the importance of building relationships. But it is not enough just to focus on the task at hand and the results you want. It is through relationships with people that we learn and grow and, ultimately, produce the desired results.

PARTNERING WITH A MENTOR

How do you and your mentor develop a relationship? You get to know each other, you build trust, you establish the expectations and agreements that define the mentoring relationship, and you set goals.

GETTING TO KNOW EACH OTHER

Building a relationship starts with getting to know each other. How do you do this? You might suggest meeting in an informal setting, such as your company cafeteria or a restaurant, for lunch or breakfast. It's nice to get away from the office environment: a less formal setting will help you relax and be more comfortable, and it's more conducive to open communication. Here are some tips for communicating and getting to know each other:

- *Ask questions.* What's the best way to learn more about another person? Asking questions, of course. Ask about your mentor's job, goals and ambitions, and experiences. But don't limit your questions to professional life. Find out about favorite hobbies or sports, and ask about your mentor's family.
- *Share information about yourself.* Self-disclosure helps another person get to know you. Let your mentor know what your goals and ambitions are. Tell her about your work role and your work experience. Share information about your family, friends, hobbies, and so on.
- *Find common interests.* In your discussion, you may discover something you both have in common—say, fishing. This gives you a common bond and another conversation topic. People usually feel more comfortable around people with whom they have something in common.

These communication tips are especially important when your mentor is different from you in some significant way (gender, ethnicity, age, and so forth). If there are such differences between you, make a special effort to help your mentor feel comfortable. A popular buzzword is *inclusion,* which refers to creating an environment where people feel not only that they belong but also that they are valued, and this is especially important in mentoring relationships.

Let's say your mentor comes from another culture. Show interest in it. Find out as much as you can about his culture by reading books or articles or doing research on the Internet. Ask your mentor about his culture. What are the customs and traditions? This interest will demonstrate to your mentor that you value him. It also helps you understand how to relate to him.

BUILDING TRUST

Another crucial component of an effective mentoring relationship is trust. Building trust is about building a safe, inclusive environment where people feel free to be themselves and be vulnerable. When people trust each other, they can be authentic and vulnerable; they feel free to share concerns and to give open, honest feedback. A mentee is not going to learn anything if he is not able to admit his deficiencies.

Listening and sharing build trust. If you truly listen to another individual, it shows him that he is important and valued. When you disclose information about yourself, especially your challenges or mistakes, people feel safer with you.

Table 2, on the next page, lists types of behavior that build and break trust. Review the list. Focus on building trust, and try to avoid breaking trust. What are some areas of building trust that you need to work on?

A sure way to break trust is to divulge something told to you in confidence. Confidentiality is a must for effective mentoring partnerships. Because of your mentor's position, she may be privy to information that others don't have. She may share inside information with you on the condition that it go no farther, or you may share concerns or issues involving your manager or co-workers, and of course you don't want your comments to get back to them.

The private and confidential nature of a mentoring relationship makes it safe to be authentic. Unlike a boss, a mentor does not write a performance evaluation, so you can feel freer to share your challenges and deficiencies, knowing that your remarks won't show up in a performance review.

Trust doesn't develop overnight. Building trust takes time. Some people will trust you until you give them reason not to trust you, but most of the time you need to earn people's trust. Building trust requires regular interaction. Trust between you and your mentor will be built over time as your mentor experiences your consistent behavior.

The responsibility rests with you. You need to demonstrate trust-building behavior in order to prove yourself trustworthy. Only trustworthy people can build trusting relationships.

TABLE 2 Building (or Breaking) Trust

The Person Who Builds Trust	The Person Who Breaks Trust
Listens	Ignores, doesn't listen
Shares thoughts and feelings	Hides thoughts and feelings
Keeps promises	Breaks promises
Acts in a consistent manner	Acts unpredictably
Accepts other people	Is critical and judgmental of other people
Is open to new ideas and information	Is closed-minded and opinionated
Builds people up	Insults and ridicules others
Cooperates	Competes
Focuses on the positive	Stresses deficiencies and negatives
Is authentic, transparent	Is manipulative, has a hidden agenda
Treats people as individuals	Categorizes and stereotypes people
Matches actions to words	Sends mixed signals
Admits mistakes	Blames others
Keeps confidences	Divulges confidential information

SETTING EXPECTATIONS AND NEGOTIATING AGREEMENTS

The next phase in building a mentoring relationship involves setting expectations and negotiating agreements. It is important to talk early in a mentoring relationship about how you're going to work together. This sets the foundation for your partnership.

When things don't go well in a relationship, often the difficulty can be traced to unclear expectations or false assumptions. How many times have you simply assumed something, only to find out that someone else didn't have the same assumption or expectation? This happens frequently in marriage; in a two-career couple, for example, the wife may expect all chores to be shared equally, whereas her husband may expect his wife to take on all the household chores, just as his mother did when he was growing up. Likewise, inappropriate expectations may also find their way into a mentoring relationship, as when a mentee assumes that he is next in line for a promotion because his mentor is in a position of power. Here are some other inappropriate expectations:

- The mentor will approach his friends or associates to advance the mentee's cause.
- The mentor will be available at any time of the day or night to respond to the mentee's needs.
- The mentor will have all the answers.

Assumptions like these can get us into trouble.

Expectations need to be explicitly discussed and agreed on. Typically, agreements are verbal, although written agreements may be used in formal mentoring programs. Expectations and agreements may touch on the following areas:

- The roles of mentor and mentee
- Decisions about whether the mentor will act as a sounding board, a coach, or an advisor
- The extent to which the mentor will open doors for the mentee and help the mentee make connections with others
- The mentee's responsibility for setting goals and tracking his or her own progress
- The need for the mentee to have a prepared agenda in hand when meeting with the mentor

If mentor and mentee are in the same organization, they will also need to discuss the role of the mentee's supervisor. How will the supervisor be involved, if at all? Will the mentee let his or her supervisor know about the mentoring relationship or keep it private? Will the mentee benefit more by involving the supervisor?

It is possible for a mentee to involve a supervisor and gain his or her support for the mentoring relationship. For example, when I mentored Danielle, a young woman in my organization, she decided to involve her manager and get his input about her development needs. The development goals on which Danielle and I worked were the same ones that were included in the formal developmental plan for her job; therefore, she effectively gained her manager's support for our activities because he saw their value to her job. His support came in two forms: funds for training classes, and time away from the job for Danielle to meet with me. Danielle kept her manager apprised of our work and her progress. The manager's involvement proved beneficial in Danielle's case, but there are situations when involving a manager may not be so helpful—for example, when a mentee is pursuing a career change, and the manager is territorial and fearful of losing a valued employee.

You and your mentor need to discuss some operating principles, such as the ones listed here:

- *Duration of the partnership:* How long will you agree to work together? For six months? For one year? Until you achieve your developmental goals?
- *Meeting logistics:* How often will you meet? Monthly? Weekly? Biweekly? How long will your meetings last? Thirty minutes? One hour? Longer? When will you meet? For breakfast or lunch? During work hours? Where will you meet? At one or the other's office? In the cafeteria? At a restaurant or coffeehouse? Who will set the meetings up?
- *Confidentiality:* How will confidential information be treated? Is everything assumed to be confidential, or only what is explicitly stated to be confidential?
- *Preferences or constraints:* How do you prefer to be reached? On your business phone line? On your cell phone? By voice mail? By e-mail? Do you have any scheduling preferences or constraints?

Do you have any other constraints (frequent travel, family needs, time limitations)?

You may think that arrangements like these are rather formal, but mentoring partners often tell me that reaching agreement on such issues really got the partnership off to a good start and helped things go more smoothly.

SETTING GOALS

Set specific goals for what you want to accomplish with your mentor's help. No one has unlimited time, and goals will help you bring a focus to the relationship, one your mentor will appreciate. It's best if your goals are written down; that way, you're more likely to achieve them. They should also be linked to a timetable.

Remember the business or career goals that you set in Chapter Three? Review your goals. Put them in writing, and give them deadlines. Then communicate your goals to your mentor. Tell him what you hope to accomplish and why it is important to you. Get his input and feedback. What skills do you need in order to accomplish your goals? Having done the groundwork, you will already have some idea of the areas in which you want to develop. Your mentor may have additional suggestions for you.

To discuss your goals, write them down in the context of a development plan (see Worksheet 15, on the next page). Your plan should include your development objectives, measures, development activities, and a time frame that is realistic for you.

Let's say you're an internal technical consultant. You want to become an independent consultant offering technical expertise to clients, and you hope to accomplish this goal within the next year. As an internal technical consultant, you already have the technical skills, but do you have the business skills required for self-employment? What about marketing and selling skills? Financial management skills? With your mentor's help, identify the development objectives (no more than three) that you will need to meet in order to achieve your business or career goal. If you want to develop marketing and selling skills, how will you measure success? Will your definition of success include creating your own marketing materials? Gaining three new clients? Make your goals and objectives specific and measurable.

WORKSHEET 15 Development Plan

Career goal:

Development Objective	Measure	Development Activities	Time Frame
1.			
2.			
3.			

Ask your mentor what she thinks her own strengths are, and explore how she can help you in those areas. Together, brainstorm some development activities for each development objective. These activities can range from reading an article to shadowing your mentor on the job; the possibilities are endless. Your mentor might recommend classes or some books. She might provide coaching and feedback. She could introduce you to other experts, or you could gain the experience you need by helping her with a project. For example, I once mentored a man who wanted to get into training and development. He had the necessary education but lacked experience, so he helped me do an evaluation study of a learning center. We worked together on each phase of the project; for instance, he reviewed the survey questions and did the number crunching, and together we reviewed the results and conducted the data analysis.

Finally, we discussed recommendations. He gained valuable learning and experience, and I received help on my project.

When you set timetables for achieving your goals, choose dates that are realistic for you. This completes all of the components of your development plan. See Worksheet 16 for a sample development plan.

WORKSHEET 16 Sample Development Plan

Career goal: Become qualified for a project management position

Development Objective	Measure	Development Activities	Time Frame
Improve project management skills	90% positive feedback from team members and customers on next project	Attend "Project Management Fundamentals" workshop	End of first quarter, Q1
		Lead cross-functional task force	Q2 and Q3
		Get coaching from mentor	Continuous
Increase effectiveness in building support for ideas	Influence at least three peers to accept ideas	Attend "Building Support for Your Ideas" workshop	Q1
		Observe mentor in two meetings	1st meeting, Q2; 2nd meeting, Q3
		Get coaching from mentor	Continuous

Your development plan forms the basis for your mentoring partnership. The plan helps keep your relationship focused on your goals. You'll probably spend a lot of time working on your development objectives, and your mentor can review your progress periodically. This process will help keep you accountable to your goals.

The mentoring agreement and development plan provide a structure and tools for your mentoring partnership. Your past mentoring relationships may have been less formal, but structure and tools bring the relationship to the next level—what Linda Phillips-Jones, author of *The Mentee's Guide,* calls "enhanced informal" mentoring. Your taking advantage of these tools will increase the likelihood of your having a more productive relationship, and you'll be better able to focus on achieving your goals.

CONNECTING AND COMMUNICATING WITH CONTACTS

Building strong connections with people is the best way to build and grow your network. Just as it's important to get to know your mentor, it's important that you get to know your contacts by building rapport and trust. "It's about building human contact in a trusting way," says Bob McCafferty, president of McCafferty & Company Communications.

It's easy to get so busy and involved in other things that we don't take the time to build networking relationships. But if we don't, our networks will dry up, just as a cherry tree that no one remembers to water will wither and die and stop producing plump, delicious fruit. Relationships take time to develop. If you focus on nurturing and cultivating your relationships, your network will grow, flourish, and produce results—and your relationships are what lead to results.

OFFERING HELP

You need to have a genuine interest in other people and a desire to help others as well as yourself. If you have a genuine interest in people, you will naturally ask them about themselves, their work, and their families. By getting to know people, you can learn about their needs and desires.

Listen for opportunities to offer ideas, contacts, or other assistance. Through your conversation with Joe, for example, you may find out that he wants to start a college fund for his child. You can then refer Joe to a trusted financial advisor who has been helpful to you. Here are some other ways you can offer help:

- Share your expertise
- Share valuable information
- Suggest books or classes
- Give encouragement
- Provide help with a project

Think of yourself as a resource broker linking people with other people, and linking people with information and other resources. Think about the people you know who might be good contacts for others. "I'm a good broker," said the late Santiago Rodriguez, who was director of diversity at Microsoft Corporation. "I like to connect people with other people."

Think about information you have that might be helpful to others. Whenever you come across articles, classes, special promotions, and so forth, consider who in your network might find it useful. Bob McCafferty is very good at this. He frequently sends me articles on mentoring or communication.

"Networking is about the normal things your mother taught you," says Ken Coleman, executive vice president of global operations at Silicon Graphics. "Things like 'Be nice to people.'" Everyday acts of kindness and courtesy go a long way; it's the little things that can make a big difference. People remember the words of encouragement, the card you sent, or the pat on the back. Such things help build your relationships.

ASKING FOR HELP

In addition to offering help, it is important in networking to ask for help. Networking entails mutually beneficial relationships. Let your contacts know what you need, what you want, and what type of help would be of support.

Your needs are important—important enough for you to ask for help. And other people generally want to help; they want to contribute. In fact, they feel flattered or honored when you acknowledge their expertise. One thought that can get in the way is "I should be able to figure this out myself," but no one is an island. We are all interdependent; no one person knows everything. Terry Paulson, psychologist and author, says, "Everyone knows something better than I do."

Here are some tips for making effective requests:

- Be assertive, and ask for what you want or need.
- Be clear about what you want.
- Be specific in your request.
- Ask with no strings attached.

Here are some examples of requests:

- "Can you recommend any good printing services?"
- "I need to hire an administrative assistant. Do you know of anyone who would be qualified and interested?"
- "I'm looking for a job change and am interested in working for your company. Would you be willing to pass my résumé on to your finance manager?"
- "Do you know of anyone else who might be interested in my services?"

KATHLEEN BARTON Before getting the contract for this book, I approached a published author, Connie Neal, to see if she would be willing to share with me any tips on working with a publisher. Connie has lots of experience writing and working with publishers, since she has written more than thirty books. She agreed to my request, and we met for breakfast. Not only did I get tips on working with a publisher, Connie also shared her framework and method for writing her books. We ended up spending two hours together, and in that time I got more value than if I had paid to attend a full-day workshop.

You never know what you'll get if you just ask. One thing is for certain: if you don't ask, the answer will always be no. You get nowhere by avoiding the risk of asking. Asking for and offering help both belong to the mutual exchange of networking. Through such interactions we build stronger connections with others that lead to mutually beneficial relationships.

USING BUSINESS CARDS

Your most important tool in building networking relationships is your business card. The first rule is always to carry your business cards with you. Always be prepared; you never know when an opportunity may come up. Carry some of your cards in your purse, your briefcase, your planner, and your glove compartment. I know a woman who even keeps some in her jogging suit. You don't want to be caught without your business cards; people without cards are missing opportunities.

Have a system for handing out and collecting business cards. Keep your own cards in one pocket, and use another pocket to collect others' cards. (I suggest you keep your cards in the same pocket as your hand preference.) If you follow this practice, you will avoid handing out the business card of the person you just met!

Exchange cards at the appropriate time. There are two schools of thought on this. Some people suggest that you exchange cards with another person as soon as you meet. If you exchange cards immediately, however, it interrupts the flow of conversation. I think that cards should be exchanged only when there's a need (for example, you want to keep in touch or get together with someone else, or you have some information to exchange).

Susan RoAne, author of *The Secrets of Savvy Networking,* shares an example of "a fellow who attended an event, arrived after everyone was seated and placed his card in front of each attendee, said a few words, and then left the event." RoAne states that "events are opportunities to meet people and exchange cards . . . *after* an exchange of conversation, *not instead of it.* Will this "card shark" be remembered? Most likely, but not pleasantly. Will he receive any follow-up calls or referrals? Unlikely."

Go for quality, not quantity, when collecting business cards. It doesn't matter how many cards you collect; what counts is the quality of the connections you make. It's better to have fewer cards from people you're likely to keep in touch with than pockets bulging with cards from people you won't even remember a week from now.

FOLLOWING UP

Have you ever shuffled through your business cards and come across one you didn't recognize? Maybe you couldn't even remember who gave it to you, or where you met this person. To avoid this situation, track business cards when you receive them. Take a moment to jot a note on the back of the other person's card. You might indicate where you met the person and/or the connection you made. For example, if you find out that the other person, like you, enjoys playing tennis, make a note of it, or note a physical characteristic that will help you remember him or her. And if you promised to send information, write a reminder on the back of the card.

When you get back to your office, sort through your cards. You'll want to follow up with some of the people. With other people, you'll want to file their cards in a card holder or enter their names and contact information into your contact database. Again, do follow up with people whenever you have promised to do so; show people that you are sincere and trustworthy. You can follow up in a number of ways:

- Mail a letter or note
- Send an article or newspaper clipping
- Call to make a lunch date
- Phone with the name and number of someone you recommended
- Send your promotional materials
- Call to thank someone for attending a function, and invite him or her to the next one

Follow up within a week. Timely follow-up helps other people remember you and increases the possibility of continued networking. Make following up a priority, and avoid missing some wonderful opportunities.

SUMMARY

- Building strong relationships with people is the best way to build your mentor network.
- You and your mentor can get to know each other by asking questions, sharing information about yourselves, and looking for common interests.
- Trust is crucial to mentoring and networking relationships. Focus on trust-building behaviors.
- Set expectations with your mentor, and discuss how you are going to work together. Some important topics to discuss are the roles of mentor and mentee, meeting logistics, confidentiality, and any preferences and constraints.
- Set goals for what you want to accomplish with your mentor's help, and write your goals in a development plan. This plan should include your development objectives, measures, development activities, and a time frame.
- Listen for opportunities to offer help. Offer help by sharing ideas, information, or expertise; by suggesting resources, such as people, books, or classes; and by giving encouragement and moral support.
- Let your contacts know what you need, what you want, and what type of help would be of support. Make effective requests by being clear and specific and asking for what you want, with no strings attached.
- Your most important tool in building relationships is your business card. Always carry your business cards with you, and exchange cards with others only when there is a stated reason.
- Follow up with people. Mail a letter, a note, an article, or promotional materials, or call to schedule a lunch or thank someone for attending a function.

LEARNING TOOLS

1. Discuss the topics in the Mentoring Agreement (Worksheet 17) with your mentor.
2. Use Worksheet 15 (page 88) to create a development plan.
3. In the next week, listen for opportunities to offer help, and offer some form of assistance to three people.
4. At your next business or networking event, strive to make three high-quality connections. Exchange business cards with these people, and follow up with them within the next week.

WORKSHEET 17 Mentoring Agreement

Mentor: ______________________ Mentee: ______________________

Phone: ______________________ Phone: ______________________

E-mail: ______________________ E-mail: ______________________

Term of Partnership: ____

What expectations do you have of each other? What is the mentor's role? What is the mentee's role?

How involved, if at all, will the mentee's supervisor be? What role should he or she play?

How often, when, and where will the two of you meet?

How will confidential information be treated?

What preferences or constraints does each of you have?

CHAPTER 7

MAINTAINING RELATIONSHIPS

Now that you understand how to build effective mentoring and networking relationships, let's focus on how to maintain these relationships. Like a cherry tree, relationships need to be nurtured and cared for. And just as nurturing the growth of a tree is analogous to building a relationship, doing the required maintenance work on a car is analogous to maintaining a relationship. What happens if you don't give your car regular tune-ups? Your car eventually wears down, and in the meantime it doesn't run efficiently. Your mentoring and networking relationships need regular maintenance, too.

Maintaining a relationship, like building one, requires initiative. This means keeping in touch on a regular basis, expressing appreciation, and giving back. These requirements apply to mentoring and networking relationships alike. They help these relationships grow and thrive.

Mentoring relationships will be more focused and intense than most networking relationships. Therefore, an additional element—learning—is needed to help the relationship thrive. Learning will help you grow and achieve your goals, and your mentor will thrive with the knowledge that he or she has aided in your development.

KEEPING A MENTORING RELATIONSHIP STRONG

In Chapter Six, we saw the importance of establishing a relationship with a mentor by getting to know her, setting expectations, discussing how you're going to work together, and creating development goals and plans. Once you've done the initial work to develop the relationship, there are several things you can do to keep the relationship going strong. Here are the key elements of maintaining a mentoring relationship:

- Managing the relationship
- Respecting your mentor and your mentor's time
- Accepting feedback and advice nondefensively
- Internalizing and applying what you learn
- Showing appreciation
- Giving back to your mentor

MANAGING THE RELATIONSHIP

In order for the mentoring relationship to continue and thrive, you need to take responsibility. After all, this relationship is for your development, and so you, as a proactive mentee, should manage the mentoring process and relationship. This means setting up meetings, maintaining regular contact with your mentor, and conducting process checks along the way.

As the mentee, you should be setting up meetings or at least taking responsibility to ensure that they are scheduled. It helps if you can have regularly scheduled meetings (for example, every other Wednesday for lunch). That way, if either of you needs to cancel, you already have another date on the calendar.

Maintaining regular contact with your mentor is the best way to keep the relationship going. You should also go to your scheduled meetings with an agenda. Identify the things you want to talk about with your mentor. This will help both of you make the best use of your time together.

It's helpful to conduct process checks along the way. How are you doing? Are you making progress on your developmental plan? Are you learning new things? Are you getting what you want out of the relationship? And what about your mentor? Does she feel that her time with you is well spent? How is the partnership working? Is there open communication between the two of you? Are needs being met on both sides? Refer to the Mentoring Process Outline in Worksheet 18.

WORKSHEET 18 Mentoring Process Outline

1. Development activities completed to date
   Action: **Result:**

2. Knowledge/skill gain

3. Other benefits I've received

4. Strengths of mentoring partnership

5. Ways that this mentoring partnership could be more effective

RESPECTING YOUR MENTOR AND YOUR MENTOR'S TIME

Throughout your relationship, show respect for your mentor. Observe such common courtesies as returning phone calls, showing up for meetings, being on time, and being prepared.

In particular, be considerate of your mentor's time. Your mentor is investing his time to help you. Think about it. How much is your time worth? Odds are that your mentor's time is worth a lot more, since he is typically in a higher position. Initially, your mentor is making a larger investment in the relationship than you are; the mentor may not see the benefits until later.

You can respect your mentor's time by following these tips:

- When arranging meetings, try to work around your mentor's schedule, to make the meetings convenient for him.
- Be flexible in scheduling.
- Be on time for meetings; don't keep your mentor waiting.
- Keep to the scheduled time, and don't run over unless your mentor suggests it.
- Try not to cancel a meeting unless it's absolutely necessary. If you must cancel, let your mentor know as soon as possible, and let him know the reason.

In general, try to be sensitive to your mentor's needs in all your interactions.

ACCEPTING FEEDBACK AND ADVICE NONDEFENSIVELY

Be eager to learn. Be open to new ideas, feedback, and suggestions. One of the best ways to learn is through feedback. If we don't know how we're doing, then how can we improve?

"I think it's important to have mentors who are straightforward and tell me what they think," says Linda Hoffman, managing partner at PricewaterhouseCoopers. That way, she says, if there's a problem, "I have an opportunity to fix it."

Proactive mentees see feedback from their mentor as a gift. It can sometimes be uncomfortable, but it also can be very helpful. "My mentor gave me objective feedback and constructive criticism," says Joe Kilkenny, deputy associate director at Lawrence Livermore National Laboratories. "Our interactions were often painful but productive. I have a better view of myself. As a result, I learned the value of feedback and give constructive feedback to the people who work for me."

Openly discuss the topic of feedback early in your mentoring partnership. Encourage your mentor to give you feedback. Tell her that you value her perspective and want to hear her honest assessment of your performance. Tell your mentor the form in which you prefer to receive feedback. If you value directness and honesty, then tell her that you would like to hear direct, honest, straightforward feedback. Or you might ask your mentor to be honest with criticism but also sensitive to your feelings; tell her that you also want to hear what you're doing well.

Ask for suggestions for improvement. Be specific when asking for feedback. Instead of asking, "How am I doing?" ask how effective your presentation to management was, or how you performed on the sales call. This approach will encourage your mentor to be more specific and helpful in her feedback.

Finally, receive feedback nondefensively. Don't take it personally. Unfortunately, women in particular have a tendency to take things personally and let feedback affect their self-worth. It helps to triangulate the discussion; that is, the two of you look at the issue. Focus on your behavior or your performance, not on you as a person. People with high self-esteem are better able to accept constructive criticism.

Seriously consider all advice and suggestions. Accept advice with an open mind. Be willing to try new things. Try out suggestions when you can, and share the results with your mentor. Knowing how things are going will make her better able to provide continued help. If you never follow through on suggestions, or if you forget to share the results of trying them, your mentor is likely to get frustrated and feel that she's wasting her time.

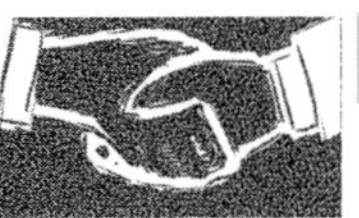

MICHELLE HOWARD Frustration was eating away at Michelle Howard, a procurement program manager. Her career seemed to be at a standstill. She sought help from a mentor, Christine Bouten, who was a middle manager in Michelle's organization.

Christine gave Michelle some strong feedback. It wasn't easy for Michelle to hear. She learned that her negative communication patterns were holding her back in her career. For the first time, she was able to hear and understand how she was coming across to others. They perceived her as demanding and insensitive.

Michelle accepted and internalized the feedback, and she took it to heart. She enrolled in communications classes and got coaching from her mentor. In time, she was able to change her communication patterns, and she greatly improved her interactions with others. As a result, more opportunities opened up for Michelle. She eventually got the promotion she wanted. In fact, she has been promoted twice.

By accepting feedback and suggestions nondefensively, you aid your learning and growth. You also provide reinforcement for your mentor to continue offering help. By the same token, if you don't accept feedback and suggestions, your mentor may move on to a more receptive mentee.

For example, Linda Roth, a technology systems manager, has mentored a number of new managers. Her first mentoring relationship didn't work out because her mentee wasn't able to be honest about herself; she wasn't willing to look at her weaknesses. "I got dissatisfied," says Linda. "It wasn't worth my time." Linda eventually discontinued the relationship.

INTERNALIZING AND APPLYING WHAT YOU LEARN

Learning starts with the right attitude. You need to have the desire to learn. As with receiving feedback, you need to be open, willing, and eager to learn. Be curious and inquisitive. Ask questions. Be like a sponge: soak up all the knowledge and information you can from your mentor.

In order to make the most of your mentoring experience, it is important to capture, internalize, and apply what you learn. Here are some steps for doing that.

ASK YOURSELF WHAT YOU'VE LEARNED After each learning activity or meeting with your mentor, ask yourself what you've learned. As soon as possible after the experience—ideally, no more than three hours afterward—do a mental review of what you learned so as not to lose it. What was significant? What were the key insights you gained? To reinforce your learning, record it in a journal.

ASK YOURSELF HOW YOU CAN APPLY WHAT YOU'VE LEARNED How can you apply what you've learned? Let's say you learned from your mentor how to ask questions that uncover a customer's needs. You can apply this learning by using the same technique with your next potential customer. Record in your journal how you will apply what you learned from your mentor. Be specific. Write down what you will do and when you will do it. What can you put into practice right away? The sooner you have a chance to apply your learning, the better.

TELL YOUR MENTOR WHAT YOU'VE LEARNED AND HOW YOU PLAN TO APPLY IT Discuss with your mentor what you learned—what was significant about it, and how it can help you. Tell your mentor how you plan to use the particular information, process, technique, or skill. Better yet, teach someone else what you've learned: when you teach someone else, you internalize it for yourself and reinforce your learning. In fact, one of the best ways to learn is to teach someone else.

Such a process of reflection, recording, and sharing helps increase your learning and retention. It forces you to think about what you've learned and identify the key points. If you write down what you've learned and tell your mentor, you will do better at retaining it. It's not so much what you learn as what you retain that is important. By writing down how you will apply your learning, you increase your motivation and commitment, and by telling your mentor how you're going to apply your learning, you become accountable. This also increases your motivation, since you don't want to let your mentor down.

Once you've done this, you're more likely to follow through. After you apply your learning, let your mentor know the results. What happened when you asked probing questions of your potential client to determine his needs? Were you successful? Keep your mentor apprised of your progress. Ask for additional coaching.

Following through on commitments is crucial to maintaining a strong relationship with your mentor. The biggest complaint I hear from mentors is about lack of follow-through. There's nothing worse for a mentor than giving a mentee an assignment that the mentee fails to do. Mentors get discouraged when mentees don't do what they say they are going to do. If a mentor doesn't see action, he feels that he's wasting his time and will probably stop offering help. Therefore, follow through on everything you commit yourself to with your mentor.

When you internalize and apply your learning, you gain more from the mentoring experience. You also strengthen the relationship with your mentor. Your mentor will be excited to see your learning and growth. When he sees results, he will be even more motivated to continue giving help. Your mentor is making an investment in you, and seeing the results of his efforts can be very satisfying and rewarding. According to Chip Bell, author of *Managers as Mentors,* "When a protégé gets promoted or an author's book does well, I have a sense of amazement and pride that I had a part in it."

SHOWING APPRECIATION

Show appreciation for everything your mentor does for you. Give thanks in person, leave a voice mail message expressing your thanks, or write a note. Don't take your mentor's help for granted. Don't you enjoy it when people express their gratitude? You feel valued and appreciated, and so does your mentor.

Give your mentor positive reinforcement. Compliment or praise your mentor. Be specific when giving praise or positive feedback. What in particular does your mentor do well? What specifically have you found helpful? Let your mentor know how much you appreciate her reviewing your proposal. Tell her how helpful her ideas are and how you've incorporated them. With this kind of positive feedback, your mentor will be more likely to continue her positive behavior, and that means you're more likely to continue receiving her help.

Another way to show appreciation is to give a small gift or memento. It doesn't need to be expensive. It could be a card, a framed quotation, or a framed picture of the two of you. The important thing is that it be meaningful to your mentor. Personal gifts are generally more meaningful. One mentee I know baked her mentor chocolate chip cookies as a way of showing appreciation; she knew that they were his favorites.

When you express gratitude, your mentor will feel valued, appreciated, and validated. This is one of the best ways to strengthen your relationship and keep it going strong.

GIVING BACK TO YOUR MENTOR

As your mentoring relationship progresses, you'll be in a position to give back to your mentor. In a mentoring relationship, you, as the mentee, enjoy most of the benefit. As you gain knowledge and expertise, however, you'll be in a better position to offer help to your mentor. The mentoring relationship can be a reciprocal one, and when your mentor also enjoys its benefits, it is more likely to keep going strong.

Look for ways to give back to your mentor. For example, offer information and feedback, or share your views. Learning can go both ways, so your ideas and views can give your mentor a broader perspective. If you and your mentor work in different organizations, you can bring an outside perspective and may be able to provide valuable information or feedback. Likewise, because many senior-level managers don't get much feedback, and because people at the rank-and-file level can keep an ear to the ground, you can let your mentor know how his initiatives are being received if you both work in the same organization. You may also have expertise in an area where your mentor has none. Terry Paulson, a psychologist and author, describes how he was able to give back to his mentor: "My proudest moment was when my mentor asked me to use what I had developed in his programs."

You can also give back by offering to help with one of your mentor's important projects. This is an opportunity for you to learn by doing, and your mentor will benefit from your assistance.

Sally Donahe, command sergeant major in the Massachusetts National Guard, had an opportunity to work with her mentor, Michael, on writing an application for the Army Communities of Excellence Award (similar to the Malcolm Baldridge National Quality Award). They worked for hours on end, collecting data and evaluating strengths and areas for improvement. Sally even put two weeks of her personal time into the project.

The hard work paid off when the National Guard placed first in its category, earning a $25,000 cash award. In the process, Sally learned time management, patience, and discipline. She later had the opportunity to become an Army Communities of Excellence examiner herself and was sent to Heidelberg, Germany, for her first assignment.

You can also give back by supporting your mentor in public. Support her ideas or proposals in meetings. Talk positively about your mentor when you're with other people. Compliment her in public. Refer to her achievements. Giving a public show of support for your mentor validates her and helps her career, too.

KEEPING IN TOUCH WITH CONTACTS

Just as it's important to show appreciation and give back to your mentors, it's important to behave the same way toward your network of contacts. Networking, as we've seen, involves reciprocal relationships, a give-and-take.

"If you network only when you want something, that's not networking," says Ken Coleman, executive vice president of global operations at Silicon Graphics. "It's called begging."

If you're always on the receiving end and don't give back to your network, then your network is going to dry up fast. You have to keep in touch. Regular contact will help you maintain your network.

Think about it. Let's say you have an important need, and after going over your list of contacts you decide that Joe is the person in the best position to help. But you haven't had contact with Joe for two years. How comfortable are you going to feel asking him for help?

With networking, you need to "tend the flame" as Betty Sproule, marketing manager at Hewlett-Packard Company, puts it: "A relationship can die through inattention. Think of a candle. Candles can burn a long time. But if it's windy"—that is, if the flame is disrupted—"it can be extinguished."

The strategies for strengthening and maintaining your relationships are to stay in touch, to show appreciation, and to give back. (These strategies are not mutually exclusive, of course; there are ways to show appreciation and give back that also keep you in touch.) Here are several methods for keeping in touch:

- Scheduling in-person meetings
- Making phone calls
- Mailing notes and cards
- Sharing articles and clippings
- Giving gifts

IN-PERSON MEETINGS

Personal interaction is best. Nothing helps strengthen a relationship more than face-to-face contact. But it is also the most time-consuming way to stay in touch.

There are certain people, your primary contacts, with whom you'll want to get together periodically. It's always nice to meet for a meal: breakfast, lunch, or dinner. And since you won't have time to meet all your contacts for lunch every month, set priorities. Decide which contacts are the most important ones, and make plans to get together with them at least once every three months, if possible.

If you travel frequently, take the opportunity to see contacts who live in the cities you visit. For example, I frequently do business in and around San Francisco. I have a number of contacts in the Bay Area, and when I'm in town I often take my contacts out to dinner; I seldom dine alone.

PHONE CALLS

A phone call is the next best thing to being there. Phone calls offer several advantages over written notes and letters. A phone call allows two-way personal communication. Even if you get the other person's voice mail, he or she gets to hear your vocal inflections. Your warmth and enthusiasm can come across in your voice to make a positive impact.

There are several purposes for phone calls. You might call for one of the following reasons:

- *Reconnecting.* Are there people you need to reconnect with? Maybe you haven't talked to someone for a while. With a phone call, you can let her know you're thinking of her and wondering how things are going in her life.
- *Giving contacts or referrals.* You can call to give someone a referral or put him in contact with someone else. The person you call will be more than happy to get the name of a potential client or supplier.
- *Offering help.* Calling just to see if you can help someone lets the other person know that she is important to you. It demonstrates caring on your part, which is especially important during the down times. If the person you're calling is out of a job, you might phone to see if you can provide any contacts or offer to be a reference. This is also a way of giving back to your network.
- *Asking for support.* Sometimes you'll want to call a contact to ask for assistance or support. This gives the other person a chance to help and give to the network.
- *Checking in.* When you call, you may not have a specific purpose in mind. You may just want to say, "I'm thinking of you." People like to know that they are remembered. Even a simple gesture like a phone call can be meaningful.

Think about the people in your contact database. Is there anyone you want to reconnect with? Do you want to say to someone, "Just thinking of you"? Is there anyone you can call to offer help or a referral?

NOTES AND CARDS

Sending notes and cards is another way of keeping in touch and showing appreciation. A note can be sent by e-mail or it can be written by hand; e-mail is certainly easier and a lot more convenient, and the advent of e-mail has allowed us to keep in touch with people more frequently.

"E-mail networking can be more extensive and quicker," says Donna Shirley, assistant dean of engineering at the University of Oklahoma and former program manager for the Mars Exploration Project at Jet Propulsion Labs. Many people use e-mail distribution lists, which allow them to send information and updates to a number of people at once.

Even though e-mail is convenient, it is not as personal as a handwritten note. Taking the time to write a personal note shows that you really care and are willing to go the extra mile. It can be a lot more meaningful than an e-mail message. A note or card can also be saved, reread, and treasured.

Think about people to whom you might want to send a note. They may be co-workers or superiors, business associates, clients or customers, vendors or suppliers, friends or neighbors. Is there someone you want to recognize, encourage, or thank? You can send notes to say any number of things:

- "Thanks for your business."
- "It was great meeting and getting to know you."
- "Thanks for the referral."
- "Congratulations on your promotion."
- "Good luck on your presentation."
- "Thanks for your support."
- "Great job!"
- "Thanks for thinking of me."

As executive vice president of global operations at Silicon Graphics, Ken Coleman frequently sends notes and e-mail. When a friend of his, A. Barry Rand, became chairman of Avis Rent-a-Car, Rand sent a letter to the Avis Chairman's Club to introduce himself. Ken, a club member, responded by sending Rand a note to wish him well and tell him how great the Chairman's Club is.

Keep notes short and sincere. A note doesn't have to take a lot of time; one to three sentences will be fine. The most important thing is that it be sincere. Let it come from your heart; your warmth and sincerity will come through in your writing. A note is a simple thing, but it can be very meaningful to the recipient.

A card is also meaningful, since you take the time to pick one out for a particular person. Write a short note inside: "Thinking of you" or "Good luck" or "Congratulations" or "Thank you." Send birthday, anniversary, and holiday cards. Some people keep special dates (such as birthdays) in their contact databases, and many businesses today send out birthday cards. What will really make you stand out is sending cards on other special days. If your client is Jewish, send her a Hanukkah card. If your friend is Irish, send him a St. Patrick's Day card. If your associate is Greek, send her a card for Greek Easter. If you know your contacts well, you know which holidays are meaningful to them. Sending special cards shows that you are thoughtful, creative, and willing to go the extra mile.

ARTICLES AND CLIPPINGS

Send articles, quotes, cartoons, or pictures from magazines and newspapers that may be of interest to your network contacts. If you've built good relationships, you know your contacts' interests and their areas of expertise. Sending newspaper and magazine clippings shows that you've listened to their interests and needs; you've thought of them and taken the time to clip an article. Because this kind of information can be helpful to a contact, sending it is another way of giving back.

Scan newspapers and magazines regularly. Be on the lookout for contacts' names or companies in the news. Local papers have business columns that highlight significant new hires and promotions. If you see one of your contacts listed, by all means send a card or a handwritten note of congratulations.

By sending a personal note, Bob McCafferty, president of McCafferty & Company Communications, reconnected with a business associate. He had seen her name in the local paper's business section when she was promoted to marketing manager at Foundation Health, and he sent her a note of congratulations. She, in turn, asked Bob to have lunch with her. He was delighted to accept, especially since they hadn't seen each other in two years.

Whenever you come across information that might be useful to others, pass it on. When you come across an interesting article, think about who might also be interested in it. When you hear of a conference or a training class, think about who might benefit from it. When you're pleased with service providers, consider who might also like to know about their services. Think of yourself as an information broker. Listen, read, and pass on information. Keep the flow going.

GIFTS

There are special times when you'll want to do more than send a note or a card. When someone deserves special recognition or special thanks, you can send a small gift along with a handwritten note. Again, a gift doesn't have to be expensive or extravagant; it's the thought that counts. Here are some gift ideas:

- A business card holder or case
- A framed quotation or cartoon
- A calendar
- A pen-and-pencil set
- Unique adhesive notes
- Stationery
- A book of special interest
- An audiocassette

Some businesses regularly give gifts for referrals. For example, Quentin Steele, an executive speaking coach, selects a unique gift (e.g., a travel clock, a CD, or a book) for each person whose referrals lead to new business. You may want to keep certain gifts on hand or establish a relationship with a vendor in order to make gift giving easy.

When you know a person's interests and tastes, you can choose a gift that will be truly meaningful and memorable. For example, a colleague of mine who loves golf and chocolate received an especially memorable gift from an associate: chocolate golf balls. Here are some other ideas for more personal gifts:

- A gift certificate to a favorite restaurant
- Tickets to a sporting event
- Tickets to a play or concert
- An arrangement of someone's favorite flowers
- A gift basket with someone's favorite foods
- Wine and cheese, chocolates, coffees, and the like

THE GIFT EXCHANGE

Everything we've discussed so far not only helps you keep in touch with contacts but also allows you to show appreciation and give back to your network. You can look at a network, with its reciprocal relationships, as a gift exchange. There are times when you are giving and times when you are receiving. The gift exchange helps keep networking relationships strong.

Do your part by giving. Give thanks, mail notes or cards of appreciation, send gifts, offer information or resources, lend assistance or support. When you do, you build a network that can last a lifetime.

SUMMARY

- The key ingredients of maintaining a mentoring relationship are managing the relationship, respecting your mentor and your mentor's time, accepting feedback and advice nondefensively, internalizing and applying what you learn, showing appreciation, and giving back to your mentor.
- Manage your mentoring relationship by setting up meetings, maintaining regular contact with your mentor, and conducting process checks (see Worksheet 18, page 101) along the way.
- Ask for specific feedback and suggestions for improvement. Listen to feedback nondefensively, and seriously consider taking all your mentor's advice and suggestions.
- To capture your learning, ask yourself what you've learned and how you can apply it. Then tell your mentor what you've learned and how you plan to apply it.
- Strengthen and maintain your relationships by staying in touch, showing appreciation, and giving back.
- You can stay in touch through face-to-face meetings, phone calls, the mail, and gifts.
- Make phone calls to reconnect, give referrals, offer help, ask for support, or let people know you're thinking of them.
- Send notes or cards to recognize, encourage, or thank network contacts.
- Send articles, quotes, cartoons, or pictures from magazines and newspapers that may be of interest to your network contacts.

LEARNING TOOLS

1. Do a process check with your mentor. Discuss the topics in Worksheet 18, on page 101.
2. Ask your mentor for feedback. Let him know that you value his perspective and want to hear an honest assessment of your performance. Then listen openly, and receive the feedback nondefensively.
3. Keep a learning journal. After each learning activity or meeting with your mentor, ask yourself what you learned and how you can apply it. Record your responses using Worksheet 19. Then tell your mentor what you learned and how you plan to apply it.
4. Review your contact database or file of business cards. Identify the people you should contact by phone or in person, either to reconnect or to find out how they're doing.
5. List three people you can acknowledge by writing notes. Write three notes during the coming week.

WORKSHEET 19 Learning Journal

Date:

What I learned ______________________________

____

____

How I will apply learning

Action Steps: **Dates:**

1. ______________________________
2. ______________________________
3. ______________________________

Outcome

____

____

CHAPTER 8

OVERCOMING CHALLENGES

By now you know what it means to be a proactive professional. You know how to plan your strategy; how to find, approach, and secure assistance from mentors and network contacts; and how to build and maintain effective relationships. Does that mean everything will go smoothly? Not always. There will be challenges along the way. This chapter addresses commonly asked questions, challenges and how to meet them, and do's and don'ts regarding mentoring and networking.

QUESTIONS ABOUT MENTORING

HOW MUCH TIME WILL A MENTORING RELATIONSHIP TAKE?

The time it will take depends on your motivation and the time you have available. If you're like most professionals, you're very busy and have limited time.

Fortunately, mentoring can be effective with just a few hours per month. As a general rule, you, as the mentee, should put in at least as much time as your mentor does. You will probably spend as much time outside your meetings, working on developmental activities, as you spend in meetings with your mentor. You'll need to meet more frequently at first, to build the relationship. After the initial period, you and your mentor should meet at least once a month, to keep the momentum going. The bottom line is that you get out of the mentoring relationship what you put into it.

WHAT IF A PROSPECTIVE MENTOR SAYS NO?

If a prospective mentor says no, you need to accept that answer and move on. There are plenty of other prospective mentors out there. The key is to not take it personally. It could very well be that the prospective mentor just doesn't have the time right now.

If you follow the six-step process for approaching mentors (see Chapter Five), you will be more likely to hear a positive response. The answer won't always be yes, however, so you need to be prepared if you're turned down. If you've done your homework, you'll also have other potential mentors in mind. You can then follow the six-step process with another potential mentor.

IS CHEMISTRY NECESSARY BETWEEN MENTOR AND MENTEE?

Many mentoring relationships develop naturally when chemistry is involved; that is, the mentor and mentee like and admire each other. Chemistry is definitely an asset, but you can have an effective mentoring relationship without it. You don't even have to like each other, but you do need to respect each other; then, mutual liking or even a friendship can sometimes evolve.

LINDA HOFFMAN When Linda Hoffman, managing partner at PricewaterhouseCoopers, was a senior manager, she worked with Mike on a client team. He was the engagement partner—the one who oversees the client. When Linda first met him, she didn't like him, and he didn't like her.

"We had totally different styles," she says. "I thought he was arrogant, and he thought I was uncooperative. He expected me to drop everything and pick him up at the airport."

They struggled through their first year and got to know each other better, and each decided that the other was not so bad after all.

"He saw my potential as a partner," Linda says, "and I saw that I could learn from him. I was persistent in trying to make the working relationship go well."

Mike helped Linda build relationships with clients. He created opportunities for her to meet important people, and he took her to important meetings and gave her a role.

"I learned a lot by watching him," Linda says. "We still talk on a regular basis today. We ended up not only liking each other but becoming friends."

WHAT IF MY MENTOR DOESN'T HAVE TIME FOR ME?

"My mentor has canceled our past three meetings," Paul complains. "I seem to be low on the priority list. I'm not sure what to do about the situation."

Does Paul's complaint sound familiar? What do you do when your mentor doesn't seem to have time for you?

What you do is take a proactive stance. Initiate discussion. Some mentees are reluctant to do this because they see their mentors as more important than themselves. Typically, a mentor is in a higher-level position, and a mentee may be concerned about asking for too much. But try to overcome this fear. Be bold. Communicate your concern, and discuss the issue.

Present options. If your mentor travels a lot, can you schedule virtual meetings (by phone) instead of face-to-face meetings? Can you schedule meetings more frequently, with the expectation that some will be canceled? Maybe the time is not right for your mentor, and there are too many other demands on him right now for him to be able to devote time to you. If so, then it's best to get the situation out in the open, discuss it, and make a decision to end the partnership rather than be disappointed time and again.

WHAT IF MY MENTOR DOESN'T FOLLOW THROUGH?

It may be easier and more comfortable to avoid this issue and just let it go, but if you do, and the problem persists, the relationship will eventually dissolve. My advice is to address the problem directly. Express your concern. Tell your mentor what you've observed in her behavior and how it has affected you. If you need to, go back to your initial working agreement. You may have to redefine your expectations or roles, but often just expressing your concern and establishing better communication can resolve the issue. But if you take these steps and still find that the problem exists, you may need to consider dissolving the relationship.

WHAT IF MY BOSS FEELS THREATENED?

This issue can arise when your mentor is in the same organization and your boss knows about the relationship. Occasionally a boss may feel intimidated or threatened by a mentor. Your boss may feel jealous of the time and attention your mentor gives you, or your boss may feel intimidated because your mentor outranks him. In organizations that are prone to empire building, your boss may also be afraid that your mentor will steal you away from his department.

In each case, discuss the issue with your boss. Educate your boss about your mentor's role, your own role, your goals, and what you're working on with your mentor. Point out the benefits to your boss and your department. For example, you may be learning some new skills that will help you in your current job while helping you become qualified for a promotion. Point out that, as a result of your increased knowledge and skills, you'll be able to make a greater contribution to the organization. Usually a boss feels more comfortable with a mentoring partnership after he has more information about it.

Think about appropriate ways to include your boss. For example, you can solicit his input on potential areas for your development. You can share your goals and update him on your progress. You might even consider having your boss meet with you and your mentor. If you involve your boss, he will probably feel less threatened and be more supportive.

MENTORING CHALLENGES

LIMITED TIME AND ENERGY

The biggest challenge for anyone is limited time and energy. But there are so many things that demand our attention that it's easy to lose focus.

First and foremost, mentoring requires your commitment to your own professional development. It's easy to get sidetracked by the urgent day-to-day issues and not spend time on developing yourself, but investing in your development reaps rewards over the long term, whereas focusing on day-to-day issues limits you to short-term thinking. Stephen Covey and his associates, in their book *First Things First,* make a distinction between urgent tasks that are not necessarily important and important tasks that are not necessarily urgent. You need to spend time regularly on important priorities, such as your development, that may not be quite as urgent as others. It's up to you to make that commitment.

Besides making the commitment to spend time working with a mentor, you need to determine the appropriate amount of time. What is realistic for you? Early in the relationship, discuss with your mentor how much time you're willing to spend. What constraints do you have? Be sure to communicate these, too. This will help establish your mentor's expectations.

FINDING A FEMALE (OR MINORITY) MENTOR

Women and people of color face special challenges in the workplace. Many face barriers to getting ahead in their organizations. Often a female professional will seek a female mentor who can understand the issues she faces and help her navigate the organizational maze. The same is true for many people of color who seek mentors like them, people who can understand the challenges.

It can be difficult to find female or minority mentors. For one thing, in some industries there are fewer female and minority managers and even fewer female and minority executives, and, therefore, there are fewer available to mentor. For another, some women or minority-group members may feel that they've had to work so hard to reach and maintain their levels of achievement that there's no time left over to mentor anyone. Despite these challenges, many women and people of color have been successful in finding mentors like themselves. Don't limit yourself to just your organization. Women and people of color may not have enough role models inside their organizations. Seek people outside your organization. Join a professional organization targeted specifically to women or people of color, such as the National Association of Female Executives, the National Association of Women Business Owners, Professional Women of Color, or the Council on Career Development for Minorities. If you network with groups like these, you're likely to make the connections you need and find a mentor like yourself.

"There are not many women partners in public accounting," says Linda Hoffman of PricewaterhouseCoopers. "I got involved in a 'women in business' organization. I got to know other women. Some were role models and mentors for me."

If, despite your best efforts, you are unable to find a female or minority mentor, then consider the next best thing: a male or Caucasian mentor. Just because you can't find a mentor like you, don't forgo having a mentor. By all means, search out other mentors. You can still learn a lot from mentors who are not like you.

CULTURAL DIFFERENCES BETWEEN MENTOR AND MENTEE

Mentoring partnerships between people from different cultures can present a challenge, since people from different cultures have different traditions, customs, and practices. Therefore, if you do not understand another person's culture, there is greater likelihood of misunderstanding or miscommunication. In addition, some people hold stereotypes of different cultures; they have preconceived notions of how people from different cultures behave. Stereotypes can be a block to truly understanding another person.

The solution is to have an open mind. Be willing to listen. Don't prejudge. Be open to learning from your mentor, and learn as much as you can about her culture. Try to step into her shoes and understand her life. Ask questions. When you are not sure of how to interpret something she has said, ask what she means. You might even read up on her culture or attend a cultural event with her.

BB Hill, principal consultant at Organization Development Associates, has worked with a number of people from different countries. "My preconceptions of people in Germany were that they would be more structured and task oriented, and less people oriented," says BB. "I was willing to suspend my own judgments. I found that my preconceptions were not correct."

ROMANTIC INVOLVEMENT

Male-female mentoring partnerships can be sticky because of potential romantic involvement. Always keep your mentoring relationships on a professional level!

There are precautions you can take to avoid romantic entanglements. Be very clear about your intentions at the outset. Let your mentor know that you see the relationship as strictly professional, and that you do not have any social or romantic intentions. Formalize your relationship, and set strict limits. (And if you can't set appropriate boundaries with a particular mentor, then you shouldn't get a mentoring relationship started.)

Despite your attempts to keep your relationship on the professional level, you and your mentor may still fall prey to office gossip or even slander. If this happens, let the gossips know that they are misinformed, and reinforce the fact that the relationship is a professional one. Stick to your principles, and maintain your code of ethics. Hold your head high. Rise above the gossip.

This can be such a sensitive area that you don't want to give even the appearance of impropriety. If there is a perceived potential for romantic involvement, set guidelines (for example, lunch rather than dinner meetings). Always meet in a public place, such as the office or a restaurant, rather than in a hotel room or in your home. Your reputation is not something you should risk.

If your mentor steps over the line and you feel uncomfortable about it, address the problem right away. Talk about your concerns, and if you and your mentor cannot reach an agreement, or if the problem persists, end the relationship.

REMOTE MENTORING

It can be a challenge when you and your mentor are not in the same geographical area. In this situation, remote mentoring, although a challenge in itself, can be very effective. If you can't find a mentor locally, look for a mentor elsewhere. The best mentor for you may be in another state.

For remote mentoring to be most effective, it's a good idea if you and your remote mentor can meet in person at an early stage of the partnership, to establish a connection and build the relationship. This meeting will bring greater commitment. With a face-to-face meeting as a foundation, your subsequent meetings by phone should run a lot more smoothly.

Take advantage of other technology, too. Supplement phone meetings with the use of a fax machine and e-mail. You can send each other documents in advance so that you can each review information at the same time during your meeting. You may also be able to use utilities like NetMeeting and other Web-based forms of communication, which allow both of you to view presentation slides on-screen as you meet by phone. You can share a document and each make edits to it. You can even use an electronic whiteboard to brainstorm and capture ideas. Whether you use advanced technology or not, you should create an agenda for your meetings so that you can stay focused while you're on the phone together.

MAINTAINING THE MOMENTUM

Sometimes, if time and attention are not paid to a mentoring relationship, it dwindles and eventually dissolves. How do you keep the relationship from fizzling out? How do you maintain the momentum?

First, it is very helpful to have regularly scheduled meetings. That way, if either of you needs to cancel a meeting, you already have the next one scheduled. Second, focusing on your developmental plan will help maintain the momentum. Unfocused, unstructured mentoring partnerships tend to fizzle out. Mentor and mentee may get together occasionally for coffee and a chat, but after the third meeting they run out of things to talk about.

JAN SHAW & BILL FISKE

Although Jan and Bill's mentoring relationship started off strong, it lost momentum. Jan wanted someone to test ideas with, someone she could go to when she had an issue to discuss. Therefore, when she was in the midst of a project at work, she went to Bill for ideas and advice and found them helpful. But when her project ended, Jan didn't seek further help from Bill, and the mentoring relationship fizzled out.

By focusing on your development plan, you can structure development activities throughout the mentoring partnership. A developmental focus also gives you things to look forward to, such as attending workshops or shadowing your mentor at a meeting. Mentoring partnerships that focus on the mentee's professional development are usually more effective, too.

WHEN IT ISN'T WORKING OUT

What do you do when a mentoring partnership just isn't working out? There may be personality clashes or differences in style, or maybe you're not getting much out of the relationship.

Before you decide to end it, be sure you've given it a fair shot. Your mentor may have a style different from yours, but that doesn't mean the partnership can't work. In fact, if your mentor does have a different style, it may even be helpful for you because you'll be able to see things differently, stretch yourself, and learn. That was the case with Ann Livermore, president of Business Customer Organization at Hewlett-Packard Company. Ann's mentor at Hewlett-Packard, Jim Arthur, "had the reputation of being one of the biggest ogres at HP—he was viewed as being very tough," Ann recalls. "But I learned more from Jim on how to run an operation, and he was one of the best executives at developing people."

Even after giving the relationship a fair shot, however, you may find that there are serious personality clashes. Usually a situation like this involves loss of respect, perhaps on the basis of the mentor's behavior or advice. If that happens, discuss the situation, and focus your conversation on your differences in style. This is a more tactful way to end a relationship and can avoid hurting your mentor's feelings.

When her boss made inappropriate advances, Sally Donahe, a command sergeant major in the National Guard, had a serious clash with a mentor. Her mentor, who had been a father figure to her, advised Sally not to file a complaint: it would make things harder for her in her career, he told her. "I didn't appreciate that advice," Sally says. "I lost some respect for him. I filed the complaint anyway."

It's helpful at the outset to discuss potential problems in the mentoring partnership and how they might be overcome. You and your mentor can talk about this issue when you discuss how you're going to work together.

Some mentoring pairs have what is called *no-fault dissolution,* whereby either party can end the relationship at any time if it's felt not to be working. This kind of arrangement, more common in formal mentoring programs, makes it easier to end a mentoring relationship without placing blame.

WHEN TO END IT

All mentoring relationships go through phases, and there comes a time when the mentoring relationship must end. Remember that the mentoring relationship is not meant to last forever; a mentor's presence usually accompanies a job or career transition for you. If you and your mentor don't actually separate on a physical basis, then the relationship should evolve and take on a new beginning. The mentee eventually needs to take a more independent role, and the two former mentoring partners will then relate more as peers or equals.

BB Hill recalls introducing Margaret as her mentor at a meeting. Afterward, Margaret took her aside. "Don't introduce me as your mentor anymore," she told BB, "because now we're colleagues. You have a lot to teach me. It's a two-way thing." BB had completed the mentoring cycle.

How do you know when the cycle is complete? How do you know when it's time to move on? This discussion can actually start early in your relationship. Some mentoring pairs establish a specific time frame, such as six months or one year. In that situation, it's easier to end the relationship because expectations are established at the outset.

Whether or not you establish a specific time frame, it is helpful to ask how you will know when you're successful. When you get a new job or start a new career? When you attain a certain level of skill or influence? Talk about how you will know when you've completed the mentoring relationship. This will make it easier to move on and make the transition when the time comes.

Some mentoring relationships blossom into friendships. That is not necessarily an expectation as you begin a mentoring relationship, but it's a bonus if it happens. Heather Shea, managing director of Interim Personnel Services, says of her former mentor, Tom Peters, "Now we're pals. There's mutual admiration. We're more like colleagues, but I know that I can call any time I need advice or counsel." At the very least, you have a new member of your network—someone you can go to for guidance, direction, or connections. The mentoring relationship comes full circle; you are peers, and you have a lot to offer your former mentor. The relationship evolves into a mutually beneficial one, and your previous mentor gets just as much out of it as you do, or maybe more.

NETWORKING CHALLENGES

FINDING THE TIME

How do you make time for networking when you're already so busy? Those who network find that they actually save time and become more efficient. If you have a good network, you are able to accomplish tasks and goals more quickly and with less effort.

As you practice networking, it will become part of your life. You'll come to see networking not as something you need to do, not as something that takes time away from you, but as a part of how you interact and relate to others day to day. Your networking interactions give you connections and opportunities, the return on your investment of time and energy.

DECIDING WHICH NETWORKING CLUBS OR ORGANIZATIONS TO JOIN

There are a number of networking organizations out there. How do you decide which ones are right for you?

Start by asking your colleagues and friends. The best way to find a good organization is by networking. Ask your associates what organizations they belong to. Keep your objectives in mind, and ask which organizations would best suit your needs.

Review organizations' materials. Is the organizational mission clear and in alignment with what you want to accomplish? What about the structure? Are meeting times and locations convenient? Are there opportunities to develop relationships that will help you build your business or career?

Visit an organization as a guest, and observe the members. Do people show interest in you as a guest? Do people seem excited to be there? Is there camaraderie? Does it appear that people are referring business to one another? You want to find an organization that will help you achieve your objectives, but that's not all. You also want to belong to an organization whose members you enjoy and whose meetings you look forward to.

You also need to find out what's required in terms of time and money. To get the most out of your membership, you want to be sure you can make the commitment.

OVERCOMING SHYNESS

For some people, it can be daunting to enter a room that's full of strangers. Many people, and you may be one of them, don't feel comfortable in large groups or in social situations. With practice, however, you can become more confident and adept in social situations.

Stretch yourself. Be bold. Introduce yourself to others. If this is your first time at an event, tell someone; that can be a conversation starter, and you can follow up with questions about the organization. Keep in mind that you have something in common with everyone in the room: you are all there for a purpose. Therefore, you can comment on something related to the meeting—the speaker, the topic, the people, and so on. Have a conversation starter in mind, and you'll feel more confident.

Ask questions. Most introverts are very good listeners, and this trait can work to your advantage because most people love to talk about themselves. By asking questions, you can engage and get to know another person. You may never completely overcome your shyness, but if you practice these tips, over time you'll feel more comfortable and confident when you meet new people.

GENDER DIFFERENCES

How can you be more effective in networking with people of the opposite sex? Gender differences do exist in how we communicate and network. To be more effective networkers, men and women need to be aware of these differences and work on improving their individual styles.

As Deborah Tannen explains in her book *Talking from 9 to 5,* men tend to talk with the intention of informing, so they are typically straightforward and get to the point quickly. Women, by contrast, tend to connect and bond through talking, so they talk in order to understand others better and build relationships. These two styles have their pros and cons.

Men are typically very focused on their goals. They tend to be more direct and clear in asking for what they want—information, leads, and so on. The old boys' network has fostered camaraderie among businessmen, but men can benefit from moving beyond this style to build more diverse and more inclusive networks. Men can also be more effective networkers with women if they work on their relationship-building and listening skills.

Women's strengths typically lie in their ability to relate to, connect with, and support others. They tend to be givers and helpers. They are aware of others' needs and are often willing to offer help, but many need to learn to speak up more assertively and professionally about the value they can contribute; they may feel uncomfortable touting their own accomplishments. Women also need to be more direct in how they communicate. They can be more effective networkers with men if they speak with conviction and assertively ask for what they want instead of using tag questions ("Don't you think so?") and qualifiers. Women need to balance their ability to give with an ability to ask for what they want and accept support from others.

Where gender differences and networking are concerned, what about flirting? How can you make sure you don't come across as flirtatious? You always need to be very professional in how you communicate. It's important that you be aware of how you communicate through eye contact, tone of voice, and body language. Lingering eye contact, a suggestive tone of voice, sensual body language, and touching can all be perceived as flirting. By all means, avoid suggestive remarks or sexual innuendo. Focus on topics of conversation that are appropriate in a business setting. Be professional in what you say, in your tone of voice, and in your body language.

MANAGING A LARGE NETWORK

How large a network should you maintain? Is there a maximum size for maintaining good relationships?

The size of your network depends on your ability to organize and manage it. Some people with very large networks have difficulty managing them. Santiago Rodriguez, who was director of diversity at Microsoft, told me, "I have such a large network that it is hard to be responsive."

I had the same challenge. As I got more exposure, and as people began to associate my name with mentoring, I received more and more inquiries. Human resources practitioners wanted to learn about my success with Hewlett-Packard's mentoring program. I received many requests to share information in phone interviews, some of which lasted an hour. As much as I wanted to help people, I found that if I responded to all requests, I didn't have time to do my regular job. Therefore, I found an alternative: I sent my questioners a written description of Hewlett-Packard's mentoring program and suggested that they read it and get back to me if they still had questions, which I said I would answer in a phone call that would last no more than twenty minutes.

Rather than limit the size of your network, I suggest that you set priorities for it. You probably have numerous contacts whose names you've put on mailing or distribution lists. You probably also have a much smaller core network of friends, associates, and clients with whom you're in touch on a daily or weekly basis. Each level of your network requires a different level of time and attention. DeRaffele and Hendricks, authors of *Successful Business Networking,* recommend that you establish five network categories:

1. *Primary:* people to whom you are closest, and with whom you have contact every day or every week (family members, co-workers, best clients, and friends)

2. *Secondary:* people with whom you have contact on a regular basis—say, every two to six months

3. *Dormant:* people with whom you are in contact every six to twelve months (former clients, college buddies, extended family members)

4. *Inactive:* people with whom you haven't been in contact for more than a year

5. *Mailing list:* people from whom you received business cards, or with whom you spoke, more than two years ago, with no further contact

By setting network priorities, you become more capable of managing your time in a way that honors these various levels of relationship.

KEEPING TRACK OF INFORMATION

How do you track contact information effectively? Do you find yourself searching through purses, wallets, and card cases for someone's business card when you want to make contact? Your list of contacts can be your greatest asset, but if you're disorganized, it can become your greatest nightmare. You may meet a lot of people and collect a lot of business cards, but if you don't have a way to retain and recall information about your contacts, your networking will do you no good.

There are a lot of organizational tools available. You may want to use a business card file, a planner or organizer, or contact management software. The important thing is to use the tools that work for you.

Some people prefer software because it allows them to store more information and recall it easily. Software offers a lot more flexibility than a manual system does. I use Symantec Corporation's ACT! software. It allows me to look up a contact by name, company name, city, state, or any ID or status indicator that I designate (such as client, prospect, vendor, or associate). I'm able to enter as much information as I want to on the notes page, so I can jot down important characteristics of the contact and record highlights of important conversations. This program also provides a history of each contact, including phone calls, meetings, and actions taken. There are a number of other good contact management programs on the market; it's a matter of finding one that suits your needs and pocketbook.

Having a system for organizing, tracking, and recalling contact information is essential if you want to use your network to the fullest. Whether it's computerized or manual, find a system that works for you, and avoid those piles of loose business cards.

NETWORKING DO'S AND DON'TS

Now that you know how to handle your networking challenges, let me summarize by sharing some do's and don'ts of networking. Sometimes networking gets a bad rap; some people misuse it for their own purposes. They are interested only in themselves, so they turn other people off. Their behavior is inappropriate and unprofessional, and they may not even realize that they're making a bad impression. The do's and don'ts are listed in Table 3. If you pay attention to them, you can focus on positive behavior and avoid the turnoffs.

TABLE 3 Networking Do's and Don'ts

Do	Don't
Be sincere	Be insincere
Be interested in others	Come on too strong
Listen	Interrupt
Focus on people	Be too focused on sales
Mean what you say	Make idle promises
Give individual attention	Be distracted
Ask questions	Monopolize the conversation

The do's and don'ts are best summed up with this statement: *Always treat people with respect and courtesy.* Think about how you want to be treated, and treat others the same way. Treat people with respect, and show interest in them.

BE SINCERE

Have you ever had someone tell you she would do something, and you knew she had no intention of following through? Sincerity is necessary to building a strong, trusting relationship. People who drop names and don't follow through will quickly lose credibility and trust. Networking is not about looking good. It's about building lasting relationships. The way to do that is to offer help to others because you truly care, not because you want to look good. People will respect you for your sincerity.

BE INTERESTED IN OTHERS

Coming on too strong is a turnoff to most people. Have you ever had someone, upon meeting you, immediately give you his card and try to sell to you? He's obviously not interested in you as a person; he is interested only in the sale. Effective networking requires you to show a genuine interest in other people. The best way to make sales is to build trusting relationships. People do business with people they know, trust, and like. By learning more about other people—their goals, needs, and interests—you are more likely to find opportunities to fill needs with your products or services.

LISTEN

We've all been interrupted at one time or another. Think about how you feel when someone constantly interrupts you. It can be frustrating. Focus on listening. When you listen attentively, you demonstrate that others are important and that you have heard and understood what they said. Stephen Covey, author of *The 7 Habits of Highly Effective People,* says that the greatest human need is to be understood. Listening is a gift we can give others, and when we do, others are more likely to remember us in a positive way.

FOCUS ON PEOPLE

Have you ever been approached by someone at a networking event who, having determined what you do, quickly moves on? Once she has determined that you're not a good prospect, she drops you. You probably felt brushed off and more than a little put off by this behavior. That's because networking is not selling. It's inappropriate to think of networking events as business "meat markets" and approach another person as a "piece of business." Networking events are a place to meet people, make contacts, and gather information. People whose only focus is making a sale miss out on connecting with people and building relationships. Your focus should be on people, not on sales.

MEAN WHAT YOU SAY

People often say, "Let's do lunch" or "Let's get together." They may say it without really thinking, and then they never follow up. I had a colleague who, whenever we ran into each other, would say, "We should get together for lunch sometime." I took her at her word and followed up to schedule lunch, but every time I did, she either was too busy or would cancel. I learned that people don't always mean what they say. After that experience, I've tried to suggest getting together with others only if I really mean it, and then I actually do follow up and schedule some time together.

GIVE INDIVIDUAL ATTENTION

I recall talking to someone who was distracted. He was constantly scanning the room to see who else was there. I thought I must not be very important to him, and that he probably wanted to talk to someone more important. If you give another person your undivided attention, you are more likely to make a connection and be remembered. You will never make a connection if you are too busy trying to connect with everyone except the person you're talking to.

ASK QUESTIONS

Have you ever been cornered in conversation with someone who goes on and on and on? You start feeling so trapped that you look for the first chance to break free. Some people are so enthusiastic about what they do, and about sharing it with others, that they get carried away. They may not even realize that they have monopolized a conversation. Bob McCafferty, president of McCafferty & Company Communications, says his number one challenge is to "listen, listen, listen." He adds, "Those of us in the creative business are enthusiastic. If we're not careful, we don't stop to listen. You can't learn anything if you're talking, I constantly remind myself." Conversation is meant to be a two-way exchange, not a monologue. Remember to stop yourself and listen. Focus on others. Ask questions to get to know them. Concentrate on building the kinds of relationships that you want for a lifetime.

SUMMARY

- As in any other kind of relationship, there will always be challenges in mentoring and networking relationships, but these challenges can be met, and the results will repay the effort.
- Being proactive is important in your mentoring and networking relationships so that you can avoid or overcome problems.
- Open communication is crucial in a mentoring relationship. By initiating discussion and addressing concerns openly, you can resolve most issues that arise.
- Always conduct yourself professionally in your mentoring and networking relationships.
- Much of your networking success can be summed up in the Golden Rule: always treat others the way you want to be treated yourself.

LEARNING TOOLS

1. If you have further questions regarding mentoring or networking, contact The Mentoring Group. The organization's e-mail address is mentorusa@foothill.net, and its Web site is located at www.mentoringgroup.com. Every month you will find new articles on the Web site that include ideas on mentoring and tips for mentors and mentees.

2. Identify a challenge that you are currently facing with regard to mentoring or networking. Be proactive about addressing it. Start by listing the steps you need to take, and then take the first step. Here are examples of challenges and action steps:

   Challenge: You're dealing with an issue that involves your mentor.
   Action steps:

   - Discuss your concern with your mentor.
   - Generate alternatives.
   - Decide on a course of action.

   Challenge: You need to find a tool to help you organize, track, and recall information about your contacts.
   Action steps:

   - Identify your needs in order to determine your selection criteria.
   - Ask colleagues and associates for recommendations.
   - Investigate different tools.
   - Make a purchase decision on the basis of your selection criteria.

3. Complete Worksheet 20 to assess how much you've applied the mentoring principles outlined in this book.

4. Complete Worksheet 21 to assess how much you've applied the networking principles outlined in this book.

WORKSHEET 20 Mentoring Checklist

Getting Prepared

___ Define your career or business mission statement.

___ Identify your career or business goals.

___ Determine your development objectives.

___ Identify ways in which a mentor can provide assistance.

Finding and Approaching a Mentor

___ Identify potential mentors.

  ___ Identify the characteristics you want in a mentor.

  ___ Determine where to look for a mentor.

___ Approach potential mentors and gain their commitment.

  ___ Research their backgrounds.

  ___ Make contact with them.

  ___ Make a specific request.

  ___ Meet with potential mentors.

  ___ Follow up.

  ___ Ask to meet with mentors on a regular basis.

Establishing a Relationship

___ Get to know each other and build trust.

___ Set expectations and negotiate agreements.

___ Set development goals.

___ Create a development plan.

  ___ Establish measures.

  ___ Discuss development activities.

  ___ Set a time line.

WORKSHEET 20 Mentoring Checklist (continued)

Maintaining the Relationship

___ Manage the relationship.

___ Respect your mentor and his time.

___ Accept feedback and advice nondefensively.

___ Internalize and apply what you learn.

___ Show appreciation.

___ Give back to your mentor.

WORKSHEET 21 Networking Checklist

Getting Prepared

___ Define your career or business mission statement.

___ Identify your career or business goals.

___ Determine your development objectives.

___ Identify ways in which a mentor can provide assistance.

___ Prepare for networking events.

  ___ Learn about events.

  ___ Determine what you want to accomplish by attending.

  ___ Identify people you want to meet or talk to.

  ___ Prepare and rehearse an introduction.

  ___ Identify what you have to offer.

WORKSHEET 21 Networking Checklist (continued)

Finding Contacts

___ Determine which (or what types of) people you want to meet.

___ Identify where to meet them.

___ Join organizations and attend meetings.

___ Get involved in one or more organizations.

Meeting Contacts and Establishing a Relationship

___ Approach contacts and engage them in conversation.

  ___ Find out everything you can about others.

  ___ Initiate conversations.

  ___ Introduce yourself.

  ___ Establish rapport.

  ___ Show interest in other people.

  ___ Call people by name.

  ___ Ask questions and listen.

___ Offer assistance.

___ Ask for assistance.

___ Use business cards.

___ Follow up.

Keeping in Touch with Contacts

___ Get together with contacts in person.

___ Make phone calls.

___ Send notes and cards.

___ Send articles and newspaper clippings.

___ Give gifts.

CHAPTER 9

PASSING ON THE GIFT

Networking and mentoring are your most important career management tools. As a proactive professional, you know the value of building your mentor network. You regularly initiate and maintain helping relationships. You are focused on learning and helping others.

Finding and learning from good mentors is the most critical step you can take in your career. As a proactive mentee, you've learned how to initiate multiple mentoring relationships. You've learned how to focus on your development goals, and you also understand your role in managing the relationship.

Truly successful people create and nurture a network of contacts. As a proactive networker, you understand the importance of building a lifetime network, and you make networking a priority. You know the importance of being prepared. You know your goals and the value that you bring. You've learned how to be assertive. You know how to approach people, initiate conversations, and ask for help. You've learned how to be supportive. You know how to offer help and be responsive, and you've learned the importance of being professional. Professional networkers follow through on promises.

BENEFITS OF MENTORING AND NETWORKING

People who have applied these principles have experienced the rewards. Building your mentor network can help you advance your career and build your business. The benefits of mentoring and networking are several. Mentoring can help you do all the following things:

- Gain knowledge and skills
- Be more effective in your job
- Understand organizational culture and politics
- Gain new opportunities and contacts
- Achieve greater career or business success

Mentoring played a big part in Chip Koehler's career, especially in helping him get started. Chip was fresh out of San Diego State University when he was hired at Ford Aerospace. At his on-site interview he met Don Briggs, who was soon to become his mentor. Chip says he "gained a lot of respect for him from the beginning." Don was a second-level department manager. "He kept close tabs on me," says Chip. Don reviewed Chip's reports and provided good feedback. He also made sure Chip had interesting assignments.

"After about a year on the job I wanted to see how my career could develop," Chip explained. He and Don talked, and Don said, "You really need to decide what you want to be when you grow up." He outlined options and suggested that Chip might want to go back to school.

Chip outlined a five-year plan, reviewed it with Don, and made the commitment to go back to school, a commitment that Don fully supported. Don actually took classes with Chip, even though he had several advanced degrees. Chip managed his five-year plan, and Don supported it by giving him the responsibilities and challenges that he needed. And everything actually happened according to plan!

"My five-year plan came true," Chip says. "I got responsibility and recognition. It became possible for me to go into positions that I might not have otherwise."

Don helped lay the foundation for Chip's career. Today, Chip is executive director of the International Space Station Program at Space Systems/Loral.

Networking, like mentoring, can help you get ahead in your career. Networking helps you do the following things:

- Find a job
- Get promoted
- Get your job done more quickly and effectively
- Gain new customers
- Get referrals and repeat business
- Get ahead of the competition

KEN COLEMAN

Having a very strong network helped Ken Coleman, executive vice president of global operations at Silicon Graphics, get where he is today. "Networking has helped me find employment opportunities and given me access to information for decision making," says Ken.

At one point in his career, he had left an employer. He called three people and ended up with half a dozen job offers. Ken had worked with all three, and they were now CEOs. In each case, his contact either offered him a job directly or recommended Ken to others who made job offers.

Networking also helps Ken get his job done. It gives him access to people and information. For example, one client company didn't want a new platform for its information technology infrastructure. This company wanted to retain its favorite vendor. "I knew we had a better product," says Ken, "but they were being quite rude to our sales team. I called the chief information officer of the company and explained the situation. I asked him to look into it and make sure it was fair." Silicon Graphics ended up getting the business and selling this company a thousand systems.

GIVING BACK (OR FORWARD)

Ken and Chip, among others, have benefited greatly from building their mentor networks. As we've said so many times, mentoring and networking are not a one-way street. They are about building mutually beneficial relationships. For example, when a mentor has invested a lot of time and energy into the growth of a mentee, a debt to the mentor is incurred, and the mentee can give back to the mentor. Some ways of giving back to mentors are outlined in Chapter Seven, but another way to give back is to give *forward* to another deserving mentee: you can repay the debt by mentoring someone else.

"I've had really good mentors all my life," says Dan Berg, deputy program manager at Space Systems/Loral. "I've been very blessed by people who want to help. I think mentoring is wonderful. That's why I'm trying to give back in the mentoring program. I'm mentoring eight people right now. I have been for about ten years. I'll keep my mentor's name and legacy alive as long as I'm in the aerospace business."

VAN JOHNSON Now president and CEO of Sutter Health, Van Johnson had several significant mentors who helped him in his career. The first was Ron Labott, chief executive officer at West Allis Memorial. They got to know each other when Van was in administrative residency. Ron took a keen personal interest in Van and set an example for him by getting to know the people who worked for him. "Every day he walked the halls," Van says. "He typified MBWA—management by walking around. He solved problems on the floor before they became major issues."

Ron taught Van a lot about management and leadership. He taught him how to run an organization. "I use many of the principles that he exemplified," says Van. "I still walk around today, even though I'm responsible for twenty-seven hospitals. It gives me a flavor of what's going on."

Dave Jeppson was another of Van's key mentors. Dave opened doors for Van. He offered Van a job in Idaho with a struggling hospital. Dave had confidence that Van could make this hospital profitable. "He gave me a chance to prove what I could do," Van says. "He pushed me out of my comfort zone."

Van remembers what his mentors did for him. "I pass along my learning by mentoring others. My goal is to teach them how to run something. If I've done that, then I've been successful."

In fact, Van has been very successful with his mentees. Nine years ago, Van mentored a woman who became executive vice president of one of Sutter Health's divisions, and he has taken on fifteen administrative residents over the years; ten of them are now CEOs in various places around the country. "It's fun," Van says. "I feel good that I've added back to the industry." ▮

Just as Dan and Van passed on the gift of mentoring, you can seriously consider giving back to others what you have learned. Have you been helped by mentors? Maybe you're ready to give career help to someone else.

The psychologist Erik Erikson, who studied adult life stages, concluded that we come to a stage in our lives when we either stagnate or assume full responsibility in the adult world. At this stage, we care about the next generation and want to give back to others. Those who give to others complete this life stage successfully. Ideally, however, we will all be mentors and mentees at the same time; we will be learning from people and also passing our learning on to others.

At some point, you will probably be ready to mentor others. Good resources for enhancing your mentoring skills are *The Mentor's Guide,* by Linda Phillips-Jones, and *Mentoring: How to Develop Successful Mentor Behaviors,* by Gordon F. Shea.

Currently a marketing manager at Hewlett-Packard Company, Betty Sproule had the advantage of being mentored by Jim Olson, a general manager at Hewlett-Packard. Jim shared with Betty what he had gained from his own mentor, Lew Platt, who had been CEO at Hewlett-Packard. Jim "paid forward" by mentoring Betty.

Later on, Betty had an opportunity to meet Lew Platt at a company function.

"Lew," she said, "you did a good deed, and I received the benefit."

"Really?"

"Yes. You mentored Jim Olson and helped him through some critical career decisions, and because he was grateful for that, he invested time in me."

QUALIFICATIONS OF A MENTOR

Are you ready to become a mentor? Review Worksheet 12 (page 50). How would you rate yourself? Of the qualifications listed, these three are the most important:

- *Possession of the desired knowledge, skills, and expertise:* You need to have what a mentee will find valuable. We all excel at something. What is your expertise? What experience can you share that others would find valuable?
- *Ability to listen, be a coach, and offer encouragement:* It's not enough to have a wealth of knowledge, skills, and experience; you also need "people skills."
- *Willingness to invest time and make the commitment:* The commitment of mentoring starts with the desire to help another person. Maybe you've been helped at some time in your career and you want to give the same help to someone else, or maybe you possess expertise that you're passionate about and eager to share with others. Either way, mentoring is an investment in someone else, and it takes time. You must be willing to make that commitment.

JOE KILKENNY Having being helped by mentors himself, Joe Kilkenny, deputy associate director at Lawrence Livermore National Laboratories, now makes the commitment to help with other people's career development. He gives his mentees management challenges. He pushes their development into other professional fields, and he makes a point of getting them the appropriate recognition.

Joe has developed five people, including David Bradley. Joe helped David find his first job, and he helped him get a later job at the University of Rochester. David Bradley is now a physicist at Lawrence Livermore National Laboratories. "I wouldn't be where I am today if it hadn't been for Joe," David says.

HOW TO FIND AND SELECT A MENTEE

Once you've made the commitment to mentor others, you're ready to find and select a mentee. You don't want to mentor just anyone. Your time is valuable, so you want to mentor someone who is committed and willing to make the same investment of time and energy. Your mentee should be someone who will respect your time and expertise. The following five steps will help you identify and screen potential mentees to select one who will be right for you:

- Determine what you have to offer.
- Identify the needs and characteristics of your ideal mentee.
- Spread the word that you are ready and willing to mentor others.
- Interview and qualify prospective mentees.
- Select a mentee.

DETERMINE WHAT YOU HAVE TO OFFER

Why do you want to mentor someone? What are your motives? Do you have special skills and experience that you want to share? Do you want to give back to others what you have received?

Be clear about your intentions, and then do a self-analysis. Determine your strengths and weaknesses, and be honest with yourself. What knowledge and skills do you possess? What other contributions can you make? Are you passionate about your career? Are you able to motivate someone else? Do you have interesting experiences to share? Are you well connected? Are you in a position of influence? Think about what you are willing and able to give. How much time are you willing to invest?

IDENTIFY THE NEEDS AND CHARACTERISTICS OF YOUR IDEAL MENTEE

Who would benefit most from what you have to offer? What career goals will your potential mentee have? What skills will he or she need to develop? Think about what you want from the relationship. What characteristics in a mentee are important to you? You will probably want a mentee who is eager and enthusiastic and who will follow through on commitments.

SPREAD THE WORD

Start spreading the word about your interest in taking on a mentee. Start with your colleagues. Networking to find a mentee is similar to the process used to find a mentor. Talk to as many people as you can. Attend meetings of professional organizations or associations. Let your contacts know what type of person you are willing to work with: perhaps a young professional, just starting out in your field, who is willing to make this investment in his or her career. Once the word spreads, you'll soon find people gravitating toward you.

INTERVIEW AND QUALIFY POTENTIAL MENTEES

When you have some interested mentee prospects, you will qualify them by interviewing them. Schedule about half an hour to meet with each one and discuss the potential of working together. You want to ensure that the prospective mentee is truly interested and committed. Ask questions like these to determine whether a prospective mentee will be a good match for you:

- What are your career goals? Why did you choose this career?
- What have you accomplished so far in your career?
- What do you hope to get out of this mentoring partnership?
- What are you willing to invest in this partnership in order to reach your goals?
- How open are you to receiving direction, advice, and feedback?
- Why do you think I should mentor you?

The questions are the same whether you seek out the mentee or the mentee seeks you out. Chip Bell, author of *Managers as Mentors,* says that when a prospective mentee approaches him for help, he asks questions to test the person's commitment. He also asks himself, "Am I the right person?"

SELECT A MENTEE

The final step is to select a mentee on the basis of your interviews. Keep in mind the needs and characteristics that you identified in connection with your ideal mentee. Also think about which of the prospective mentees you would most like to spend time with.

YOU GET BY GIVING

You've probably heard the old saying "What goes around comes around." This is another way of saying that what you give comes back to you. Donna Fisher, author of *People Power,* calls it the "boomerang effect." When you give, contribute, and offer support, it will come back to you. Opportunities will come your way. Janet Drez's experience with networking demonstrates this principle.

JANET DREZ

Janet had met Andrea at an association meeting. She and Andrea developed a professional relationship, and for about five years they periodically worked on projects together.

One day while Janet was on vacation, Andrea called to ask for some quick help with a project. Janet's assistant, Darlene, took the call and then phoned Janet, who suggested that Darlene go ahead and help Andrea with the project. "Darlene did a great job," Janet says.

Later, Andrea got a request from a contact who needed administrative help, and she referred the contact to Darlene, who took the assignment. "Since Darlene was doing such a fine job," Janet says, "they asked her if she could refer them to anyone with marketing/PR expertise. Knowing that's my background, Darlene recommended they contact me. Talk about full circle! What you give does come back to you."

Even though you give a lot to one person, the return may come back to you from someone else, so you don't have to keep score;

that's not what it's about. Trust the process, and make sure you're doing your part to give.

"I help people whenever I can be a genuine help," says Betty Sproule of Hewlett-Packard. "I'm not counting the balance. I freely give it away. I never ask what this person could do for me, even though networking is reciprocal. I have no expectation of return, but it always comes back, multifold. It's like yeast; it multiplies. If I give today, the future will be brighter."

Harvey MacKay, author of *Dig Your Well Before You're Thirsty,* helps make the future brighter for young people. He enjoys giving career advice and counseling. "It's become my avocation," he says. "I've done this with over a thousand young people in the course of a lifetime, and I get enormous satisfaction from hearing from them and about them later on as their careers progress."

Sometimes the return comes back in a tangible way, such as increased business; sometimes the return is in our own feelings of tremendous satisfaction. Winston Churchill has been quoted as saying, "We make a living by what we get; we make a life by what we give."

MAKE MENTORING AND NETWORKING PART OF YOUR LIFE

The more you work on building mentoring and networking relationships, the more natural it will become for you. Eventually, it will become part of the way you think and relate to people. It will become part of your life.

If everyone practiced the principle of giving to others to build mutually beneficial relationships, the world would be a better place to live. Roz Hudnell, worldwide community education manager at Intel, says, "The true value of networking is that it helps you live your life better."

Just think about what would happen if everyone both served as a mentor and became a mentee! It would perpetuate a positive cycle of mentoring those who will follow us, who in turn would mentor others. When we share our learning with others, we're more able to solve our problems, and we make better decisions. We're more effective at what we do, and we're more successful in achieving our goals.

SUMMARY

- Building your mentor network can help you advance your career and build your business.
- Pass on the gift of mentoring. You can repay the debt to your mentor by mentoring someone else.
- The most important qualifications of becoming a mentor are possession of the desired knowledge, skills, and expertise; the ability to listen, coach, and give encouragement; and the willingness to spend the time involved in mentoring.
- To find and select a mentee, first determine what you have to offer and identify the needs and characteristics of your ideal mentee. Then spread the word that you're looking for a mentee, and interview prospective mentees.
- What you give comes back to you. Even though you give a lot to one person, the return may come back to you from someone else.
- Make mentoring and networking part of your life. If everyone strove to build mutually beneficial relationships, the world would be a better place to live.

LEARNING TOOLS

1. Make a list of how you have benefited thus far from mentoring. From networking.
2. Assess yourself as a potential mentor using Worksheet 12 (page 50).
3. Identify what you have to offer a mentee, and the needs and characterisitics of your ideal mentee using Worksheet 22.

WORKSHEET 22 Mentor Self-Assessment

What I have to offer	Needs/characteristics of mentee	Prospective mentees

REFERENCES

Bell, Chip R. *Managers as Mentors: Building Partnerships for Learning.* San Francisco: Berrett-Koehler, 1998.

Bjorseth, Lillian D. *Breakthrough Networking: Building Relationships That Last.* Lisle, Ill.: Duoforce Enterprises, 1996.

Carnegie, Dale. *How to Win Friends and Influence People.* New York: Pocket Books, 1994.

Covey, Stephen R. *The 7 Habits of Highly Effective People: Restoring the Character Ethic.* New York: Simon & Schuster, 1989.

Covey, Stephen R., Merrill, A. Roger, and Merrill, Rebecca R. *First Things First: To Live, to Love, to Learn, to Leave a Legacy.* New York: Simon & Schuster, 1994.

DeRaffele, Frank J., and Hendricks, Edward D. *Successful Business Networking.* Worcester, Mass.: Chandler House Press, 1998.

Duff, Carolyn S. *Learning from Other Women: How to Benefit from the Knowledge, Wisdom, and Experience of Female Mentors.* New York: American Management Association, 1999.

Fisher, Donna. *People Power: 12 Power Principles to Enrich Your Business, Career and Personal Networks.* Austin, Tex.: Bard Press, 1995.

Karasik, Paul. *How to Make It Big in the Seminar Business.* New York: McGraw-Hill, 1995.

Kaye, Beverly. "Shared Brain Power." *National Business Employment Weekly,* November 23, 1997.

Kelley, Robert. *How to Be a Star at Work: Nine Breakthrough Strategies You Need to Succeed.* New York: Times Books/Random House, 1998.

MacKay, Harvey. *Dig Your Well Before You're Thirsty: The Only Networking Book You'll Ever Need.* New York: Doubleday, 1999.

Phillips-Jones, Linda. *The Mentee's Guide: How to Have a Successful Relationship with a Mentor.* Grass Valley, Calif.: Coalition of Counseling Centers, 2000a.

Phillips-Jones, Linda. *The Mentor's Guide: How to Be the Kind of Mentor You Once Had—or Wish You'd Had.* Grass Valley, Calif.: Coalition of Counseling Centers, 2000b.

Shea, Gordon F. *Making the Most of Being Mentored: How to Grow from a Mentoring Partnership.* Menlo Park, Calif.: Crisp Publications, 1999.

Shea, Gordon F. *Mentoring: How to Develop Successful Mentor Behaviors.* Menlo Park, Calif.: Crisp Publications, 1992.

Tannen, Deborah. *Talking from 9 to 5 : Women and Men in the Workplace: Language, Sex, and Power.* New York: William Morrow, 1994.

ADDITIONAL READING

Cohen, Norman H. *The Mentee's Guide to Mentoring.* Amherst, Mass.: Human Resource Development Press, 1999.

Fisher, Donna, and Vilas, Sandy. *Power Networking: 55 Secrets for Personal and Professional Success.* Austin, Tex.: Bard Press, 1992.

Phillips-Jones, Linda. *The New Mentors and Protégés: How to Succeed with the New Mentoring Partnerships.* Grass Valley, Calif.: Coalition of Counseling Centers, 1997.

RoAne, Susan. *The Secrets of Savvy Networking: How to Make the Best Connections for Business and Personal Success.* New York: Warner Books, 1993.

Sjodin, Terri, and Wickman, Floyd. *Mentoring: The Most Obvious Yet Overlooked Key to Achieving More in Life Than You Dreamed Possible.* New York: McGraw-Hill, 1997.

INDEX